SUCCESSFUL
VEGETABLE COOKERY

GOOD HOUSEKEEPING
STEP-BY-STEP COOKERY

SUCCESSFUL
VEGETABLE
COOKERY

Guild Publishing/Ebury Press
LONDON

Consultant editor: Jeni Wright
Editors: Caroline Schuck and Anne Charlish
Design: Mike Leaman
Illustrations: John Woodcock and Kate Simunek
Photography: Martin Brigdale
Stylist: Andrea Lampton
Cookery: Susanna Tee, Maxine Clark, Janet Smith

Cover photograph: Salad Elona (page 69), Artichokes with Hollandaise Sauce (page 17)
and Spinach and Mushroom Pancakes (page 29)

Filmset by Advanced Filmsetters (Glasgow) Ltd

Printed and bound in Italy by
New Interlitho, S.p.a., Milan

CONTENTS

COOKERY NOTES

Follow either metric or imperial measures for the recipes in this book as they are not inter-changeable. Sets of spoon measures are available in both metric and imperial size to give accurate measurement of small quantities. All spoon measures are level unless otherwise stated. When measuring milk we have used the exact conversion of 568 ml (1 pint).

* Size 4 eggs should be used except when otherwise stated.

† Granulated sugar is used un-less otherwise stated.

● Plain flour is used unless otherwise stated.

OVEN TEMPERATURE CHART

°C	°F	Gas mark
110	225	$\frac{1}{4}$
130	250	$\frac{1}{2}$
140	275	1
150	300	2
170	325	3
180	350	4
190	375	5
200	400	6
220	425	7
230	450	8
240	475	9

METRIC CONVERSION SCALE

LIQUID			SOLID		
Imperial	Exact conversion	Recommended ml	Imperial	Exact conversion	Recommended g
$\frac{1}{4}$ pint	142 ml	150 ml	1 oz	28.35 g	25 g
$\frac{1}{2}$ pint	284 ml	300 ml	2 oz	56.7 g	50 g
1 pint	568 ml	600 ml	4 oz	113.4 g	100 g
$1\frac{1}{2}$ pints	851 ml	900 ml	8 oz	226.8 g	225 g
$1\frac{3}{4}$ pints	992 ml	1 litre	12 oz	340.2 g	350 g
For quantities of $1\frac{3}{4}$ pints and over, litres and fractions of a litre have been used.			14 oz	397.0 g	400 g
			16 oz (1 lb)	453.6 g	450 g
			1 kilogram (kg) equals 2.2 lb.		

KEY TO SYMBOLS

1.00* Indicates minimum preparation and cooking times in hours and minutes. They do not include prepared items in the list of ingredients; calcu-lated times apply only to the method. An asterisk * indicates extra time should be allowed, so check the note below symbols.

Chef's hats indicate degree of difficulty of a recipe: no hat means it is straightforward; one hat slightly more complicated; two hats indicates that it is for more advanced cooks.

£ Indicates a recipe which is good value for money; £ £ indicates an expensive recipe. No £ sign indicates an inexpensive recipe.

✳ Indicates that a recipe will freeze. If there is no symbol, the recipe is unsuitable for freezing. An asterisk * indicates special freezer instructions so check the note immediately below the symbols.

309 cals Indicates calories per serving, including any sugges-tions (e.g. cream, to serve) given in the ingredients.

SUCCESSFUL VEGETABLE COOKERY

Meals without meat and fish—as this book illustrates so beautifully—can be varied and interesting as well as healthy. You will find a wealth of recipes using vegetables as their main ingredient, all of which are so colourful, tasty and economical that you'll only wish you'd made more of vegetables in the past. Every recipe has its own full-colour photograph to tempt you, and there are also step-by-step illustrations to guide you swiftly through the cooking methods, suggestions for making up menus, plus helpful hints and useful tips. From delicious soups and starters to substantial main courses, summery salads, cold dishes and unusual hot vegetable accompaniments, the book provides chapter after chapter of exiciting vegetable dishes for you to try.

The tinted section at the back of the book contains lots of information on all aspects of vegetable cookery, plus a handy collection of basic recipes, how to choose and store vegetables; how to prepare them and which equipment to use; information on the more unusual pulses, grains, nuts and seeds, and an invaluable chapter on the healthy aspects of eating vegetables and vegetarian diets. Presentation and garnish, which are so important when cooking and serving vegetables, are covered in the chapter on finishing touches.

Soups and Starters

Vegetables make such light and refreshing soups and starters. From cool split pea soup to unusual Middle Eastern dips and exotic Indian samosas, you will be amazed just how versatile vegetables can be.

ICED SPLIT PEA AND MINT SOUP

| 1.30* | £ | ✳ | 242 cals |

* plus at least 4 hours chilling

Serves 4

225 g (8 oz) green split peas

2 litres (3½ pints) unsalted
 vegetable stock or water

1 cooking apple

25 g (1 oz) fresh mint leaves

juice of ½ lemon

2 bay leaves

salt and freshly ground pepper

150 ml (¼ pint) single cream,
 to serve

fresh mint sprigs, to garnish

1 Rinse the split peas well under cold running water. Put the peas in a large saucepan and add the stock or water.

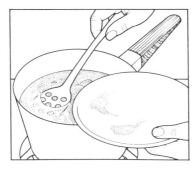

2 Bring the liquid slowly to the boil, then skim off any scum with a slotted spoon.

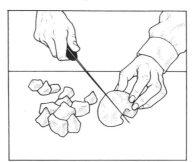

3 Peel and core the cooking apple, then chop roughly. Add to the pan with half of the mint, the lemon juice and the bay leaves.

4 Half cover the pan with a lid and simmer gently for about 1 hour or until the peas are very tender.

5 Discard the bay leaves. Work the soup to a purée in a blender or food processor, then work through a sieve into a bowl, pressing with the back of a metal spoon. Add the remaining mint, with salt and pepper to taste. Leave until cold, then chill in the refrigerator for at least 4 hours, preferably overnight.

6 To serve, taste and adjust seasoning, then pour into individual bowls and swirl with cream. Garnish with fresh mint sprigs. Serve chilled.

Menu Suggestion
This prettily-coloured soup makes the perfect starter for a summer meal. Serve with wholemeal or granary rolls and butter. Chilled dry white wine is the ideal drink.

**ICED SPLIT PEA
AND MINT SOUP**

Split peas are most often associated with warming winter soups like the famous split pea and ham soup from northern England. This recipe for iced split pea soup is cool and delicate, quite the opposite. You can buy two types of split pea, green and yellow, and either can be used for this soup, but the green ones give a prettier colour. Both kinds have been split through the middle, as the name suggests, then skinned. This makes them easy to cook like split red lentils—perfect for puréed soups such as this one.

LETTUCE SOUP

| 1.15 | £ | ✳ | 178 cals |

Serves 4

350 g (12 oz) lettuce leaves

100 g (4 oz) spring onions, trimmed

50 g (2 oz) butter or margarine

15 ml (1 tbsp) plain flour

600 ml (1 pint) vegetable or
chicken stock

150 ml ($\frac{1}{4}$ pint) milk

salt and freshly ground pepper

soured cream, to finish (optional)

1 Chop the lettuce leaves and
spring onions roughly. Melt
the butter in a deep saucepan, add
the lettuce and spring onions and
cook gently for about 10 minutes
until very soft.

2 Stir in the flour. Cook,
stirring, for 1 minute, then add
stock. Bring to the boil, cover and
simmer for 45 minutes to 1 hour.

3 Work the soup to a purée in a
blender or food processor, or
rub through a sieve. Return to the
rinsed-out pan and add the milk
with salt and pepper to taste.
Reheat to serving temperature.
Finish with a swirl of soured
cream, if liked.

Menu Suggestion
Lettuce soup has a pretty colour
and delicate flavour. Serve as a
summer starter, with Melba toast.

CAULIFLOWER BUTTERMILK SOUP

| 0.50 | £ | 258 cals |

Serves 6

900 g (2 lb) cauliflower
1 large onion, skinned
50 g (2 oz) butter or margarine
1 garlic clove, skinned and crushed
15 ml (1 tbsp) plain flour
900 ml ($1\frac{1}{2}$ pints) milk
2 eggs, beaten
300 ml ($\frac{1}{2}$ pint) buttermilk
pinch of freshly grated nutmeg
salt and freshly ground pepper
25 g (1 oz) flaked almonds
15 ml (1 tbsp) chopped fresh
   parsley

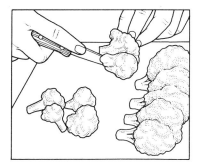

1 Cut away any green stalks from the cauliflower, and cut it into small florets. Roughly chop the onion.

2 Melt 25 g (1 oz) of the butter in a saucepan. Add the onion and garlic and fry for 3–4 minutes until golden.

3 Stir in the flour. Cook, stirring, for 1 minute, then add the milk and cauliflower.

4 Bring to the boil, cover and simmer for 25–30 minutes or until the cauliflower is very soft.

5 Work the soup to a very smooth purée in a blender or food processor, or rub through a sieve.

6 Return to the rinsed-out pan. Beat in the eggs, buttermilk, nutmeg and salt and pepper to taste. Reheat very gently, without boiling.

7 Melt the remaining butter in a small frying pan. Add the almonds and parsley and fry until the nuts are golden. Scatter over the soup before serving.

Menu Suggestion
Serve this creamy, nutritious soup for a quick lunch. Wholemeal baps and a selection of cheeses would go well with it.

CARROT AND CARDAMOM SOUP

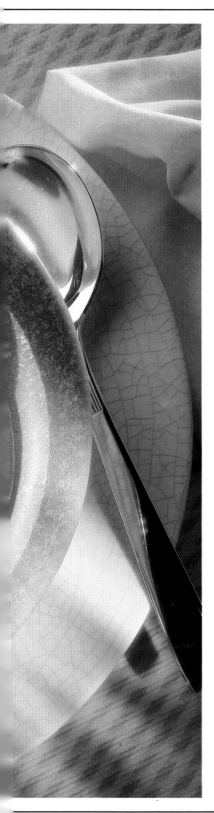

| 0.35 | £ | ✳ | 151 cals |

Serves 4

200 g (7 oz) carrots, peeled

1 medium onion, skinned

50 g (2 oz) butter or margarine

10 whole green cardamoms

50 g (2 oz) red lentils

1.1 litres (2 pints) vegetable or chicken stock

salt and freshly ground pepper

parsley sprigs, to garnish

1 Grate the carrots coarsely. Slice the onion very thinly. Melt the butter in a large saucepan, add the carrots and onion and cook gently for 4–5 minutes.

2 Meanwhile, split each cardamom and remove the black seeds. Crush the seeds with a pestle and mortar, or with the end of a rolling pin.

3 Stir the cardamom seeds into the vegetables with the lentils. Cook, stirring, for a further 1–2 minutes.

4 Add the stock and bring to the boil. Cover and simmer gently for about 20 minutes, or until the lentils are just tender. Add salt and pepper to taste before serving and garnish with parsley sprigs.

Menu Suggestion
Quick to make, this nutritious soup makes a hearty lunch or early evening supper served with an Indian bread such as naan, chapati or puri. For a dinner party starter, serve with crisply fried poppadoms.

CARROT AND CARDAMOM SOUP
Cardamoms go especially well with carrots, and give this soup an exotic Indian flavour. When buying cardamoms, look for the green pods rather than the black. Green cardamoms have a fine flavour, whereas the black ones are coarser and may overpower the delicate sweetness of the carrots in this recipe. Delicatessens and supermarkets sell green cardamoms, but for freshness it is best to buy them from an Indian grocer who has a fast turnover. Buy them loose in small quantities as they quickly go stale and lose both their aroma and flavour. Store them in an airtight jar in a dark cupboard, and do not remove the seeds from the pods until you are ready to use them.

VEGETABLE AND OATMEAL BROTH

| 1.00 | £ | ✳ | 98–146 cals |

Serves 4–6

1 medium onion, skinned

175 g (6 oz) swede, peeled

2 medium carrots, peeled

1 medium leek, trimmed

40 g (1½ oz) butter or margarine

25 g (1 oz) medium oatmeal

1.1 litres (2 pints) vegetable or
   chicken stock

salt and freshly ground pepper

150 ml (¼ pint) milk

chopped fresh parsley, to garnish
   (optional)

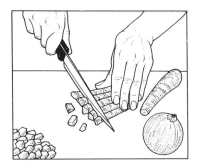

1 Dice the onion, swede and
   carrots finely. Slice the leek in
1 cm (½ inch) rings, then wash well
under cold running water to
remove any grit.

2 Melt the butter in a large
   saucepan, add the vegetables
and cook gently without browning
for 5 minutes. Add the oatmeal,
stir well and cook for a few
minutes.

3 Stir in the stock and salt and
   pepper to taste and bring to
the boil. Lower the heat, cover
and simmer for about 45 minutes,
or until the vegetables are tender.

4 Add the milk and reheat to
   serving temperature. Taste
and adjust seasoning before
serving. Sprinkle with chopped
parsley, if liked.

Menu Suggestion
Thick with vegetables and
oatmeal, this broth makes a hearty
supper. Serve with crusty
wholemeal bread or rolls.

VEGETABLE AND OATMEAL BROTH

With swede and oatmeal, this
soup has a definite Scottish
flavour. As their name suggests,
swedes came from Sweden, and
were originally called Swedish
turnips, although they were also
known as Russian turnips and
even by the name of rutabaga,
too, from their botanical name.
In the eighteenth century,
swedes were grown in Scotland
and northern England to feed
sheep and cattle. It was soon
discovered that the sweet flavour
and delicate colour of the flesh
made them suitable for human
consumption, too, and they
became a popular vegetable in
the nineteenth century. In
Scotland, swedes are still called
turnips, or 'neeps' for short,
which often causes confusion;
haggis and 'bashed neeps' are a
national dish, traditionally eaten
together on Burns Night.

ASPARAGUS WITH MELTED BUTTER

0.20	£ £	335 cals

Serves 4

450 g (1 lb) asparagus
175 g (6 oz) butter, melted

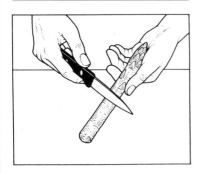

1 Rinse each asparagus stalk very gently to wash away any dirt. Scrape or shave the length of the stalk, starting below the tip.

2 Cut off the end of the asparagus stalk if it is tough and woody. Place in a bowl of cold water and prepare the rest.

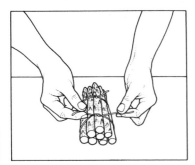

3 Trim the asparagus stalks to roughly the same length. Tie the asparagus into neat bundles of 6–8 stalks of an even thickness, heads uppermost. Secure each bundle of asparagus under the tips and near the base.

4 Put the bundles of asparagus in a special asparagus pan, or wedge them upright in a deep saucepan. Pour in enough boiling salted water to come three-quarters of the way up the stalks.

5 Cover the tips of the asparagus with a cap made of foil. Simmer gently for about 10 minutes until tender. (This way the stalks are poached while the delicate tips are gently steamed — see box.)

6 Drain the water carefully from the pan, take out the asparagus and remove the ties. Serve immediately, with the warm melted butter.

7 To eat asparagus, pick up each piece by the stalk, dip it in the butter or sauce and eat the tip and soft part of the stem. You will need napkins or finger bowls to clean your fingers afterwards.

Menu Suggestion
Serve for an elegant dinner party starter, with a chilled dry white wine — or Champagne.

ASPARAGUS WITH MELTED BUTTER
Home-grown asparagus cut within 1 hour of cooking takes even less cooking time — from 3–5 minutes. Even if you don't want to use it at once, absolutely fresh asparagus is best cooked immediately, then kept cool and used for dishes such as omelettes and gratins.

ARTICHOKES WITH HOLLANDAISE SAUCE

1.15   £ £   702 cals

Serves 4

4 globe artichokes

$\frac{1}{2}$ **lemon**

**300 ml ($\frac{1}{2}$ pint) Hollandaise Sauce
(page 149)**

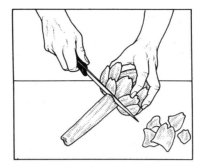

1 Break off the toughest outer leaves from each artichoke. With a sharp knife, cut off the stem quite close to the base leaves.

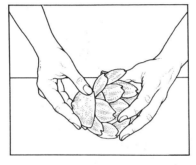

2 Trim the spiky leaf tops, according to variety, with a sharp knife or scissors. Rub the cut surfaces with the lemon half to prevent discoloration.

3 Globe artichokes have close-fisted leaves which make hideout havens for insects, particularly earwigs. Wash them well under running water or soak the whole artichokes in a bowl of cold water, to which a few drops of lemon juice or vinegar has been added, for about 30 minutes.

4 Place the artichokes in a large saucepan of boiling salted water. Simmer gently for 35–40 minutes, according to size. To test whether the artichoke is cooked, try pulling out a leaf. If it comes out easily, the artichoke is cooked. Turn the heads upside down in a colander to drain for a few minutes.

5 The 'choke' must never be eaten as the little barbs, on what would eventually become the thistle-like flower heads of the mature plant, can irritate the throat. You can easily recognise the choke: it is a mass of yellowish silky hairs arising out of a firm-textured heart. Pull out the chokes with your fingers, or scoop them out with a spoon or knife. Serve the artichokes while still hot, with the warm hollandaise sauce.

Menu Suggestion
Serve artichokes for a summer dinner party starter. No accompaniment is necessary other than a chilled dry white wine.

ARTICHOKES WITH HOLLANDAISE SAUCE

This smoky-tasting vegetable with its flower-like head comes from the Mediterranean. Avoid full-blown specimens or those with brown leaves. The leaves should be closely folded with no dry edges, and there should be no swelling at base of globe.

An extravagant way of eating a globe artichoke is to pull off the leaves entirely and eat only the delicate heart or fond. But the leaves are usually eaten too — pull out each leaf, dip into melted butter or French dressing and eat only the fleshy leaf base.

HUMMUS
(MIDDLE EASTERN CHICK PEA AND TAHINI DIP)

| 1.20* | £ | ✱* | 277–416 cals |

* plus overnight soaking and a few hours chilling; freeze without the garnish

Serves 4–6

175 g (6 oz) chick peas, soaked in cold water overnight

about 150 ml ($\frac{1}{4}$ pint) lemon juice

150 ml ($\frac{1}{4}$ pint) tahini paste

3 garlic cloves, skinned and crushed

salt

30 ml (2 tbsp) olive oil

5 ml (1 tsp) paprika

crudités, to serve (see box)

1 Drain the soaked chick peas and rinse well under cold running water. Put the chick peas in a large saucepan and cover with plenty of cold water.

2 Bring slowly to the boil, then skim off any scum with a slotted spoon. Half cover the pan with a lid and simmer gently for about 1 hour, until the chick peas are very tender.

3 Drain the chick peas, reserving 60 ml (4 tbsp) of the cooking liquid. Set a few whole chick peas aside for the garnish, then put the remainder in a blender or food processor. Add the reserved cooking liquid and half of the lemon juice and work to a smooth purée.

4 Add the tahini paste, garlic and 5 ml (1 tsp) salt and work again. Taste and add more lemon juice until the dip is to your liking, then blend in 30 ml (2 tbsp) hot water.

5 Turn into a serving bowl and cover with cling film. Chill in the refrigerator until serving time. Before serving, mix the oil with the paprika and drizzle over the Hummus. Arrange the reserved whole chick peas on top.

PAPA GHANOOYE
(ARABIC AUBERGINE DIP)

| 0.50* | £ | ✱* | 322–483 cals |

* plus a few hours chilling; freeze without the garnish

Serves 4–6

2 large aubergines

salt

2–3 garlic cloves, skinned and roughly chopped

10 ml (2 tsp) cumin seeds

100 ml (4 fl oz) olive oil

150 ml ($\frac{1}{4}$ pint) tahini paste

about 100 ml (4 fl oz) lemon juice

thin tomato slices, to garnish

crudités, to serve (see box)

1 Slice the aubergines, then place in a colander, sprinkling each layer with salt. Cover with a plate, put heavy weights on top and leave to dégorge for 30 minutes.

2 Meanwhile, crush the garlic and cumin seeds with a pestle and mortar. Add 5 ml (1 tsp) salt and mix well.

3 Rinse the aubergines under cold running water, then pat dry with absorbent kitchen paper. Heat the oil in a large, heavy-based frying pan until very hot. Add the aubergine slices in batches and fry until golden on both sides, turning once. Remove from the pan with a slotted spoon and drain again on kitchen paper.

4 Put the aubergine slices in a blender or food processor with the garlic mixture, the tahini paste and about two-thirds of the lemon juice. Work to a smooth purée, then taste and add more lemon juice and salt if liked.

5 Turn into a serving bowl, cover with cling film and chill in the refrigerator until serving time. Serve chilled, garnished with tomato slices.

SKORDALIA
(GREEK GARLIC DIP)

| 0.30* | £ | 381–572 cals |

* plus a few hours chilling

Serves 4–6

75 g (3 oz) crustless white bread

60 ml (4 tbsp) milk

6 garlic cloves

250 ml (8 fl oz) olive oil

about 50 ml (2 fl oz) lemon juice

salt and freshly ground pepper

black olives and finely chopped parsley, to garnish

crudités, to serve (see box)

1 Tear the bread into small pieces into a bowl. Add the milk, mix and soak for 5 minutes.

2 Skin the cloves of garlic, chop roughly, then crush with a pestle and mortar.

3 Squeeze the bread with your fingers, then mix with the crushed garlic. Add the olive oil a drop at a time to form a paste.

4 When the mixture thickens, add a few drops of lemon juice, then continue with the olive oil. Add more lemon juice and salt and pepper. Turn into a bowl and cover with cling film. Chill in the refrigerator and garnish with olives and parsley before serving.

VEGETABLE DIPS
Dips make good starters for informal supper parties, or to serve at a drinks party. Crudités (raw vegetables) are ideal for dipping and dunking. To serve 4–6 people: 4 carrots, peeled and cut into thin sticks, 1 small cauliflower, divided into florets, 4–6 celery sticks, halved, $\frac{1}{2}$ cucumber, seeds removed and cut into sticks, 1 red and 1 green pepper, cored seeded and sliced, 1 bunch of radishes, trimmed. Fingers of hot pitta bread can also be served.

BROCCOLI FRITTERS

| 0.20 | £ | 275 cals |

Serves 4

900 g (2 lb) fresh broccoli

salt and freshly ground pepper

plain flour, for dusting

150 ml ($\frac{1}{4}$ pint) Fritter Batter (page 157)

vegetable oil, for deep frying

300 ml ($\frac{1}{2}$ pint) Basic Tomato Sauce (page 149), to serve

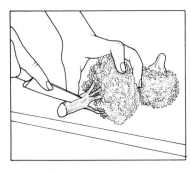

1 Trim off and discard the thick ends of the broccoli, then cut the broccoli into large florets. Cook in boiling salted water for about 10 minutes until they are nearly tender.

2 Drain the broccoli well, then dust with flour, seasoned well with salt and pepper.

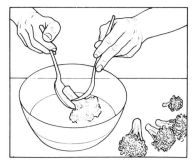

3 Lightly turn the broccoli in the batter. Heat the oil in a deep-fat frier to 180°C (350°F). Deep fry the broccoli in batches for 1–2 minutes until golden.

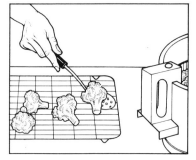

4 With a slotted spoon, transfer the fritters to a wire rack. Keep warm in a cool oven, uncovered, while cooking the remainder. Serve immediately, with hot tomato sauce.

Menu Suggestion

Broccoli Fritters make an unusual first course for an informal supper pastry. Serve with garlic bread, to help mop up the tomato sauce.

——— VARIATIONS ———

Aubergine Fritters

Cut **2 aubergines** into 1 cm ($\frac{1}{2}$ inch) slices. Blanch for 1 minute in boiling salted water, then drain well and proceed as in step 2.

Carrot Fritters

Cut **900 g (2 lb) carrots** into finger-sized sticks. Do not blanch, but proceed as in step 2.

Mushroom Fritters

Wipe **450 g (1 lb) button mushrooms** and proceed as in step 2.

Courgette Fritters

Cut **900 g (2 lb) courgettes** into 1 cm ($\frac{1}{2}$ inch) slices. Blanch for 1 minute in boiling salted water, drain and proceed as in step 2.

ASPARAGUS MOUSSES

| 1.45 | 🍴 | £ £ | 235 cals |

Serves 6

700 g (1½ lb) fresh asparagus

50 g (2 oz) butter

1 medium onion, skinned and finely chopped

30 ml (2 tbsp) lemon juice

150 ml (¼ pint) double cream

3 egg yolks

salt and freshly ground pepper

1 egg white

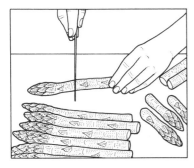

1 Cut the heads off the asparagus to a length of about 4 cm (1½ inches) and reserve. Slice the stalks into 1 cm (½ inch) lengths, discarding any particularly tough root ends.

2 Melt the butter in a medium saucepan. Add the asparagus stalks, onion and lemon juice, then pour in 200 ml (7 fl oz) water. Cover tightly and cook gently for about 30 minutes, or until the asparagus is tender.

3 Drain the asparagus well, then put in a blender or food processor with the cream. Work until almost smooth.

4 Rub the purée through a nylon sieve into a bowl to remove any stringy particles. Beat in the egg yolks with salt and pepper to taste. Whisk the egg white until stiff and fold into the asparagus mixture.

5 Spoon the asparagus mixture into six 150 ml (¼ pint) ramekins, then stand the dishes in a roasting tin. Pour in enough hot water to come half way up the sides of the ramekins.

6 Bake the mousses in the oven at 170°C (325°F) mark 3 for 40–45 minutes or until the centres are just firm to the touch.

7 Ten minutes before the end of the cooking time, steam the asparagus heads (page 16) for 5–10 minutes until tender. Serve the mousses immediately, topped with the asparagus heads.

Menu Suggestion
Asparagus Mousses make a very special dinner party starter. Serve with thin slices of wholemeal toast and butter curls. A dry sparkling white wine would be perfect, too.

CAPONATA
(ITALIAN DEEP-FRIED AUBERGINE AND CELERY WITH OLIVES AND PINE NUTS IN A TOMATO SAUCE)

1.15* £ ✳* 256–385 cals

* plus overnight chilling; freeze at the end of step 6

Serves 4–6

450 g (1 lb) aubergines

salt and freshly ground black pepper

30 ml (2 tbsp) olive oil

1 large onion, skinned and thinly sliced

2 garlic cloves, skinned and crushed

450 g (1 lb) tomatoes, skinned and roughly chopped

45 ml (3 tbsp) wine vinegar

vegetable oil, for deep frying

4 large celery sticks, trimmed

50 g (2 oz) large green olives

15 ml (1 tbsp) capers

25 g (1 oz) pine nuts

1 Dice the aubergines, then place in a colander, sprinkling each layer with salt. Cover with a plate, put heavy weights on top and leave to dégorge for 30 minutes.

2 Meanwhile, heat the 30 ml (2 tbsp) olive oil in a heavy-based saucepan or flameproof casserole. Add the onion and garlic and fry gently for about 10 minutes until soft and lightly coloured.

3 Add the tomatoes, wine vinegar and salt and pepper to taste. Simmer for about 20 minutes, breaking up the tomatoes occasionally with a wooden spoon.

4 Heat the vegetable oil to 180°C (350°F) in a deep-fat frier. Rinse the aubergines under cold running water, then pat dry with absorbent kitchen paper.

5 Deep fry the aubergines in batches until crisp and golden brown, then drain again on absorbent kitchen paper and add to the tomato sauce. Continue cooking for a further 15 minutes.

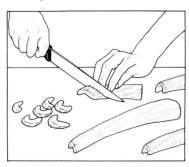

6 Cut the celery sticks diagonally into chunky pieces, then deep fry and drain as with the aubergines. Add to the tomatoes and aubergines.

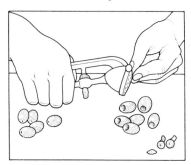

7 Stone the olives, then add to the Caponata with the capers and pine nuts. Remove from the heat and leave to cool, then chill in the refrigerator overnight. Taste and adjust seasoning before serving. Serve chilled.

Menu Suggestion
This chilled Italian starter is very rich. Serve for a dinner party or summer luncheon with chunky slices of French bread, or Italian rolls if you can get them from a local delicatessen. A chilled, dry Soave or Frascati would set off the richness of the Caponata.

VEGETABLE TARTS

| 1.30 | ⏊ | £ | ✳ | 677 cals |

Makes 4

125 g (5 oz) plain flour

salt and freshly ground pepper

150 g (6 oz) butter or margarine

1 egg yolk

1 small onion, skinned and finely chopped

2 medium courgettes, sliced

a little lightly beaten egg white

142 g (5 oz) full fat soft cheese with herbs and garlic

2 eggs, beaten

20 ml (4 tsp) chopped fresh basil or 10 ml (2 tsp) dried

fresh basil sprigs, to garnish (optional)

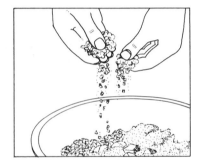

1 Make the pastry cases. Sift the flour into a bowl with a pinch of salt. Add 100 g (4 oz) of the butter in pieces and work into the flour with your fingertips.

2 Add the egg yolk and 5–10 ml (1–2 tsp) cold water and work with a palette knife until the dough draws together.

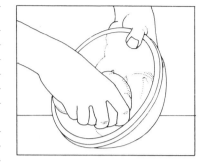

3 Gather the dough into a ball with one hand, then wrap in cling film or foil. Chill in the refrigerator while making the filling.

4 Melt the remaining butter in a heavy-based frying pan, add the onion and fry gently for about 5 minutes until soft and lightly coloured. Add the courgettes and fry over moderate heat for a few minutes, turning them frequently until they are light golden on all sides. Turn into a bowl and leave until cold.

5 Meanwhile, roll out the dough on a lightly floured surface and cut out 4 circles large enough to line 4 individual loose-bottomed 10 cm (4 inch) quiche or tartlet tins.

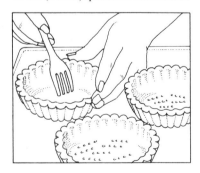

6 Place the pastry in the tins, prick the bases with a fork, then line with foil and beans. Bake 'blind' in the oven at 190°C (375°F) mark 5 for 10 minutes.

7 Remove the foil and beans, brush the pastry with the egg white and return to the oven for a further 5 minutes.

8 Put the cream cheese mixture in a bowl and beat with a wooden spoon until soft. Add the eggs and beat well to mix, then the courgettes, basil and salt and pepper to taste.

9 Divide the filling equally between the pastry cases, then return to the oven for a further 10–15 minutes, until the filling is set. Leave to stand for at least 15 minutes before serving. Serve warm, garnished with basil sprigs, if liked.

Menu Suggestion

Individual quiches make a most unusual and attractive dinner party starter. They are quite substantial, and need no accompaniment other than a chilled dry white wine such as a French Muscadet.

Served cold, the tarts make excellent cold luncheon or picnic fare, with a selection of crisp, crunchy salads, fresh granary bread or a French stick, and chilled French dry cider.

AUBERGINE SAMOSAS
(INDIAN-STYLE AUBERGINES DEEP-FRIED IN PASTRY)

| 0.45* | 🍴 | £ | 296 cals |

* plus 30 minutes to dégorge
aubergine and 30 minutes chilling

Serves 4

**1 small aubergine, about 225 g
(8 oz)**

salt and freshly ground pepper

15 ml (1 tbsp) vegetable oil

**1 clove garlic, skinned and
crushed**

1.25 ml ($\frac{1}{4}$ tsp) ground allspice

2 tomatoes, skinned and chopped

**30 ml (2 tbsp) chopped fresh
coriander**

**125 g (4 oz) shortcrust pastry
(page 156)**

vegetable oil, for deep frying

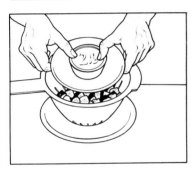

1 Chop the aubergine finely.
Place in a colander, sprinkling
each layer with salt. Cover with a
plate, place heavy weights on top
and leave to dégorge for about
30 minutes.

2 Rinse the aubergine well
under cold running water,
then pat dry with absorbent
kitchen paper.

3 Heat the oil in a heavy-based
saucepan, add the aubergine,
garlic and allspice and fry gently
for 5–7 minutes, or until softened.
Stir in the tomatoes and coriander.
Season with pepper only, then
remove from the heat and leave to
cool for 15–20 minutes.

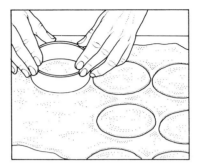

4 Roll out the pastry thinly on a
well-floured surface. Stamp
out eight 10 cm (4 inch) rounds.

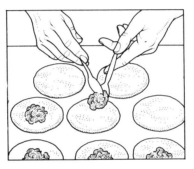

5 Spoon a little filling on each
round, brush the pastry edges
with water and fold over to form
semi-circular shapes. Press the
edges well together. Place the
samosas on a board or plate,
cover loosely and chill in the
refrigerator for 30 minutes.

6 Heat the oil in a deep-fat frier
to 180°C (350°F). Deep fry the
samosas in batches for 4–5
minutes, until golden. Drain on
absorbent kitchen paper. Serve
immediately.

Menu Suggestion
These samosas can be served as a
first course to an Indian meal,
with ice-cold lager. Alternatively,
they make an unusual snack, with
natural yogurt for dipping.

SPINACH AND MUSHROOM PANCAKES

| 1.10 | £ ✳* | 508 cals |

* freeze at step 4 after arranging in dish

Serves 4

450 g (1 lb) fresh spinach, trimmed, or 300 g (10.6 oz) packet frozen spinach

100 g (4 oz) butter or margarine

1 medium onion, skinned and finely chopped

225 g (8 oz) mushrooms, thinly sliced

25 g (1 oz) plain flour

200 ml ($\frac{1}{3}$ pint) milk

45 ml (3 tbsp) single cream

3 anchovy fillets, finely chopped (optional)

freshly grated nutmeg

salt and freshly ground pepper

8 pancakes (page 158)

60 ml (4 tbsp) fresh white breadcrumbs

30 ml (2 tbsp) chopped fresh parsley

1 Wash the fresh spinach in several changes of cold water. Place in a saucepan with only the water that clings to the leaves. Cook gently, covered, for 5 minutes until wilted, 7–10 minutes if using frozen spinach. Drain well and chop very finely.

2 Melt 50 g (2 oz) of the butter in a saucepan, add the onion and cook gently for 10 minutes until soft but not coloured. Stir in the mushrooms and cook for a further 2 minutes.

3 Sprinkle the flour over the onion and mushroom mixture and stir well. Cook gently, stirring, for 1–2 minutes. Gradually blend in the milk. Bring to the boil, stirring constantly, then simmer for 3 minutes until very thick. Stir in the spinach, cream, anchovies (if using), nutmeg and salt and pepper to taste.

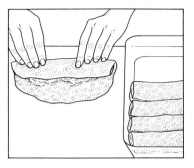

4 Divide the mixture between the pancakes and roll or fold them up. Arrange the pancakes in a buttered shallow ovenproof dish. Melt the remaining butter and pour it over the pancakes.

5 Mix the breadcrumbs and parsley together and sprinkle over the pancakes. Bake in the oven at 190°C (375°F) mark 5 for 10–15 minutes to heat the pancakes through. Serve immediately.

Menu Suggestion

These pancakes make a substantial starter. Serve a light dish such as a salad or a fish course to follow.

SPINACH AND MUSHROOM PANCAKES

For a more unusual and nutritious dish, make buckwheat pancakes. Follow the recipe as for ordinary pancakes, using half buckwheat and half wheat flour. You can use all buckwheat, but this tends to make too heavy a batter for most tastes.

Buckwheat flour is available from health food shops; it is ground from buckwheat, a seed rather than a grain which is related to dock and rhubarb and used in homoeopathic medicine as a cure for circulatory problems. Buckwheat is also rich in the B vitamins and iron, so is well worth including in your diet.

TOMATO ICE WITH VEGETABLE JULIENNE

0.45*	🍴 £ ❄	175–263 cals

* plus 6 hours freezing and 30 minutes
softening

Serves 4–6

8 very ripe tomatoes

10 ml (2 tsp) gelatine

30 ml (2 tbsp) tomato purée

30 ml (2 tbsp) lemon juice or juice of ½ lemon

a few drops of Tabasco

salt and freshly ground pepper

1 egg white (optional)

30 ml (2 tbsp) chopped fresh basil leaves (optional)

2 small leeks

2 medium carrots, peeled

2 medium courgettes

150 ml (¼ pint) Vinaigrette (page 151)

fresh basil leaves, to garnish (optional)

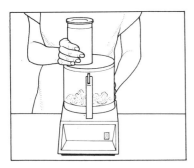

1 Put the tomatoes in a blender or food processor and work until smooth. Press the tomato pulp through a sieve into a bowl to remove the seeds and skin.

2 Put 45 ml (3 tbsp) very hot water in a small bowl and sprinkle in the gelatine. Stir briskly until dissolved, then leave to cool slightly.

3 Add the tomato purée to the tomato pulp with the lemon juice, Tabasco and salt and pepper to taste. Mix thoroughly.

4 Stir in the gelatine and chopped basil leaves (if using). Pour into a chilled shallow freezer container and freeze for about 2 hours until mushy.

5 Remove the container from the freezer and beat the mixture with a fork to break down any ice crystals. Return to the freezer and freeze for a further 4 hours. (If a creamier texture is desired, whisk the egg white until stiff, fold into the beaten mixture and return to the freezer. Freeze as before.)

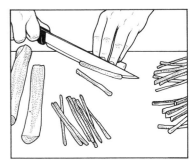

6 Meanwhile, wash the leeks thoroughly and cut into fine julienne strips of equal length. Cut the carrots and courgettes into julienne strips of the same size.

7 Bring a large pan of water to the boil and add the leeks. Blanch for 1 minute, then remove with a slotted spoon and drain on absorbent kitchen paper. Blanch the carrots in the same water for about 4 minutes, remove and drain well. Similarly, blanch the courgettes for 2 minutes and then drain them well.

8 Put the julienne of vegetables in a bowl, add the vinaigrette and salt and pepper to taste and toss gently to mix. Cover and chill in the refrigerator until required.

9 To serve, allow the tomato ice to soften in the refrigerator for 30 minutes. Arrange small scoops of tomato ice on chilled individual side plates with a 'nest' of julienne vegetables. Garnish with fresh basil sprigs, if using.

Menu Suggestion
Serve for an unusual first course, with crisp Melba toast and butter.

Main Courses

Vegetables are usually served as side dishes and accompaniments, but they make the most delicious and unusual main meals, and you don't have to be a vegetarian to appreciate them. Pizzas, pies, roulades, soufflés, quiches, curries and croquettes, are just a few of the many vegetable main courses to tempt you.

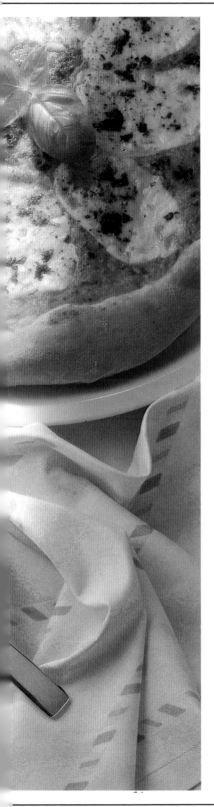

PIZZA MARGHERITA
(PIZZA WITH TOMATOES, MOZZARELLA AND BASIL)

| 1.30* | £ | ✳* | 635 cals |

* plus 1½–2 hours rising; freeze at end of step 8

Makes two 27.5 cm (11 inch) pizzas, each serving 2 people

45 ml (3 tbsp) lukewarm milk

20 g (¾ oz) fresh yeast

3.75 ml (¾ tsp) sugar

300 g (11 oz) strong white bread flour

salt and freshly ground black pepper

75 ml (5 tbsp) olive oil

1 medium onion, skinned and roughly chopped

1 garlic clove, skinned and crushed

450 g (1 lb) ripe tomatoes, skinned and roughly chopped, or 396 g (14 oz) can tomatoes

30 ml (2 tbsp) red wine or 15 ml (1 tbsp) red wine vinegar

10 ml (2 tsp) dried mixed herbs

225 g (8 oz) Mozzarella cheese, thinly sliced

20 ml (4 tsp) chopped fresh basil or 10 ml (2 tsp) dried

1 First make the pizza dough. Put the milk in a warmed jug and crumble in the yeast with your fingers. Add sugar, stir to dissolve, then stir in 60 ml (4 tbsp) flour.

2 Cover the jug with a clean tea towel; leave in a warm place for 30 minutes or until frothy.

3 Sift the remaining flour and 7.5 ml (1½ tsp) salt into a warmed large bowl. Mix in the yeast with a fork, then add 30 ml (2 tbsp) of the oil and about 90 ml (6 tbsp) warm water to draw the mixture together.

4 Turn the dough on to a floured surface and knead for 10 minutes until it is smooth and elastic. Put the dough in a large floured bowl, cover with a clean cloth and leave in a warm place for 1½–2 hours until doubled in bulk.

5 Meanwhile, prepare the tomato sauce for the topping. Heat 30 ml (2 tbsp) of the remaining oil in a heavy-based saucepan, add the onion and garlic and fry gently for about 5 minutes until soft and lightly coloured. Add the tomatoes and break up with a wooden spoon, then add the wine or wine vinegar, herbs and salt and pepper to taste. Simmer gently for about 30 minutes or until the sauce is thick and reduced.

6 Work the sauce to a purée in a blender or food processor, or alternatively, push through a sieve. Set aside.

7 Turn the risen dough on to a floured surface and roll out. Cut into two 27.5 cm (11 inch) circles, using a large plate as a guide and making the edges slightly thicker than the centres.

8 Put the pizzas on 2 oiled baking sheets. Spread the tomato sauce evenly over them, right to the edges and arrange the cheese slices on top.

9 Sprinkle the pizzas with the basil, the remaining 15 ml (1 tbsp) oil and freshly ground black pepper. Leave to prove in a warm place for about 30 minutes.

10 Bake the pizzas in the oven at 220°C (425°F) mark 7 for 25 minutes, or until the topping is melted and bubbling. Swap the baking sheets over halfway through the cooking time. Serve hot, warm or cold.

Menu Suggestion
Pizzas make filling family suppers served with a mixed salad. Crisp lettuce or endive, with sliced fennel, raw peppers and onion rings, are a good combination of salad ingredients. For an informal supper party, serve with a bottle of Chianti Classico.

WHOLEMEAL VEGETABLE PIE

| 1.00* | £ | ✳* | 767 cals |

* plus 1 hour cooling and 15 minutes
chilling; * freeze at step 7 before
brushing with beaten egg

Serves 4

3 medium leeks, trimmed

275 g (10 oz) swede, peeled

225 g (8 oz) turnip, peeled

4 medium carrots, peeled

100 g (4 oz) butter or margarine

225 g (8 oz) large flat mushrooms,
  sliced

25 g (1 oz) plain flour

300 ml ($\frac{1}{2}$ pint) vegetable stock
  (page 148)

175 g (6 oz) Cheddar cheese, grated

30 ml (2 tbsp) chopped fresh herbs,
  e.g. parsley, chives, thyme,
  marjoram or 10 ml (2 tsp) dried

salt and freshly ground pepper

175 g (6 oz) Wholemeal Shortcrust
  Pastry (page 157)

beaten egg, to glaze

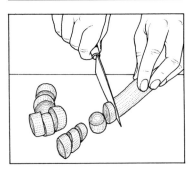

1 Cut the leeks into 2.5 cm
(1 inch) lengths, then wash
well under cold running water to
remove any grit. Cut the swede,
turnip and carrots into small bite-
sized chunks.

2 Melt the butter in a large
saucepan, add the prepared
vegetables and fry over moderate
heat for about 10 minutes until
turning golden brown. Add the
mushrooms and cook for a further
2–3 minutes.

3 Sprinkle in the flour and cook
gently, stirring, for 1–2
minutes. Gradually blend in the
vegetable stock. Bring to the boil,
stirring constantly, then simmer
for 5–10 minutes or until the
vegetables are just tender.

4 Remove the pan from the heat
and stir in the cheese, herbs
and salt and pepper to taste. Pour
into a 1.1 litre (2 pint) pie dish and
allow to cool for about 1 hour.

5 Roll out the pastry on a
floured surface. Cut out a thin
strip long enough to go around the
rim of the pie dish. Moisten the
rim with water and place the strip
of pastry on the rim.

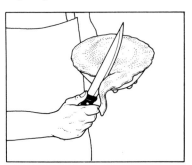

6 Roll out the remaining pastry
to cover the pie. Moisten the
strip of pastry on the rim of the
dish, place the lid on top, trim off
any excess pastry and press to seal.

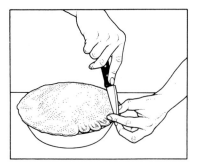

7 Knock up and flute or crimp
the edge. Decorate the top
with any pastry trimmings and
brush with beaten egg. Chill in the
refrigerator for 15 minutes.

8 Bake the pie in the oven at
190°C (375°F) mark 5 for 15–
20 minutes until lightly browned.
Serve hot.

Menu Suggestion

Serve this vegetarian main course
with 1 or 2 green vegetables such
as French beans, Brussels sprouts
or stir-fried spring greens. Jacket-
baked potatoes would also go well
with the pie, for those who are
really hungry.

**WHOLEMEAL VEGETABLE
PIE**

Mushrooms are most nutritious,
and a useful vegetable to include
in a vegetarian diet because they
contain more protein than any
other vegetable and are also
extremely rich in vitamins B1,
B2 and B6, and in the minerals
potassium, copper and
phosphorus. The Chinese have
long known that mushrooms
have health-giving properties,
and use dried mushrooms
extensively in their cooking. For
this recipe, choose the flat or
'open' mushrooms as they have a
good flavour. The smaller button
and cup mushrooms can be used
and have the same nutritional
value, but they are a little bland
for a vegetable pie.

SPINACH ROULADE

| `1.00` 🍴 `352 cals` |

Serves 3–4

900 g (2 lb) spinach, trimmed, or 450 g (1 lb) packet frozen spinach

4 eggs, size 2, separated

pinch of freshly grated nutmeg

salt and freshly ground pepper

25 g (1 oz) butter or margarine

1 medium onion, skinned and finely chopped

100 g (4 oz) curd cheese

50 g (2 oz) Gruyère cheese, grated

30 ml (2 tbsp) soured cream

Tomato Sauce, to serve (page 149)

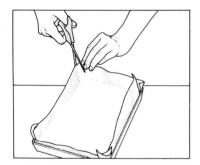

1 Grease a 35.5 × 25.5 cm (14 × 10 inch) Swiss roll tin and line with non-stick baking parchment. Set aside.

2 Wash the fresh spinach in several changes of cold water. Place in a saucepan with only the water that clings to the leaves. Cook gently, covered, for about 5 minutes until wilted or until thawed, about 7–10 minutes, if using frozen spinach.

3 Drain the spinach well and chop finely. Turn into a bowl and allow to cool slightly for about 5 minutes, then beat in the egg yolks, nutmeg and salt and pepper to taste.

4 Whisk the egg whites until they form stiff peaks, then fold into the spinach mixture with a large metal spoon until they are evenly incorporated.

5 Spread the mixture in the prepared tin. Bake in the oven at 200°C (400°F) mark 6 for 15–20 minutes, until firm.

6 Meanwhile, prepare the filling. Melt the butter in a saucepan. Add the onion and fry gently for about 5 minutes until soft and lightly coloured. Remove from the heat and stir in the cheeses, soured cream and salt and pepper to taste.

7 Turn the roulade out on to greaseproof paper, peel off the lining paper and spread the roulade immediately and quickly with the cheese mixture.

8 Roll the roulade up by gently lifting the greaseproof paper. Serve hot, cut into thick slices, with the tomato sauce.

Menu Suggestion
Serve for a weekend lunch dish with new potatoes tossed in butter, or jacket-baked potatoes topped with soured cream and snipped chives.

SPINACH ROULADE

The curd cheese used in the filling of this roulade is a medium fat soft cheese made from semi-skimmed milk. It is naturally soured, without the addition of rennet. It has a good, firm texture, ideal for a filling such as this roulade which has to keep its shape when rolled up. Cream cheese or full fat soft cheese has a similar texture and could be used instead but it is much fattier so best avoided. Many supermarkets and delicatessens now sell continental-type soft cheeses in small tubs or cartons. Called 'quark', 'fromage frais' and 'fromage blanc', these are low in fat and excellent.

VEGETABLE JALOUSIE

| 1.30* | 🍳 | £ | ✳* | 818 cals |

* including cooling time for the filling; freeze before baking at end of step 9

Serves 4

3 medium leeks, total weight about 450 g (1 lb), trimmed

4 medium new carrots, peeled

600 g (1¼ lb) fresh broad beans, shelled, or 350 g (12 oz) frozen

salt and freshly ground pepper

25 g (1 oz) butter or margarine

50 g (2 oz) plain flour

300 ml (½ pint) milk

100 g (4 oz) Caerphilly or Wensleydale cheese, grated

45 ml (3 tbsp) grated Parmesan cheese

1.25 ml (¼ tsp) ground mace

10 ml (2 tsp) chopped fresh summer savory or 5 ml (1 tsp) dried

400 g (14 oz) frozen puff pastry, thawed

a little beaten egg, to glaze

1 Slice the leeks thickly, then wash well under cold running water to remove any grit. Scrub the carrots and slice thinly.

2 Parboil the broad beans in boiling salted water for 4 minutes. Remove with a slotted spoon and set aside. Add the carrots to the water and parboil for 2 minutes only. Remove with a slotted spoon and set aside with the carrots. Parboil the leeks for 1 minute and reserve the blanching water.

3 Melt the butter in a clean pan, add the flour and cook gently, stirring, for 1–2 minutes. Remove from the heat and gradually blend in the milk. Bring to the boil, stirring constantly, then simmer for 3 minutes until very thick and smooth. Add the cheese, mace and salt and pepper to taste.

4 Remove the cheese sauce from the heat and fold in the vegetables. Cover the surface of the sauce closely with cling film, then leave until cold.

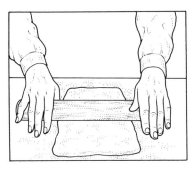

5 Meanwhile, roll out half of the pastry thinly on a lightly floured surface to a 30.5 × 23 cm (12 × 9 inch) rectangle. Place on a wetted baking sheet.

6 Stir the 30 ml (2 tbsp) of the reserved blanching water and the savory into the cold filling, then spread over the pastry on the baking sheet to within about 1 cm (½ inch) of the edges. Brush the edges with water.

7 Roll out the remaining pastry to a slightly larger rectangle than the first. Fold in half lengthways.

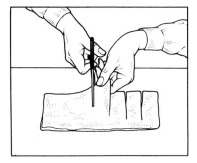

8 With kitchen scissors, cut through the double thickness of the pastry 6 times at 5 cm (2 inch) intervals.

9 Unfold the pastry and place over the top of the filling. Press the edges firmly to seal, then flute or crimp.

10 Brush the pastry with beaten egg, then bake in the oven at 220°C (425°F) mark 7 for 30 minutes until golden brown. Serve hot, cut into slices.

Menu Suggestion

Vegetable Jalousie is rich and filling. Serve with a tomato and onion salad, or a salad of crisp chicory, orange and walnut tossed in a dressing of walnut oil and cider vinegar.

VEGETABLE LASAGNE

| 1.20* | £ | ✳* | 635–1008 cals |

* plus time for making tomato and cheese sauces; freeze before baking at end of step 5

Serves 4–6

75 ml (5 tbsp) olive or vegetable oil

1 large onion, skinned and roughly chopped

1–2 garlic cloves, skinned and crushed

1 large green pepper, cored, seeded and chopped

1 large red pepper, cored, seeded and chopped

450 g (1 lb) courgettes, trimmed and sliced

40 g ($1\frac{1}{2}$ oz) butter or margarine

450 g (1 lb) mushrooms, wiped and sliced

600 ml (1 pint) Tomato Sauce (page 149)

salt and freshly ground pepper

1.25 ml ($\frac{1}{4}$ tsp) freshly grated nutmeg

600 ml (1 pint) Coating Cheese Sauce (page 148)

225 g (8 oz) lasagne (see box)

50 g (2 oz) Parmesan cheese, freshly grated

1 Heat 30 ml (2 tbsp) oil in a heavy-based frying pan. Add the onion, garlic and peppers and fry gently for about 10 minutes until they are softened.

2 Add the courgette slices in batches and fry for about 5 minutes until lightly coloured, turning them frequently and adding more oil as necessary. Remove the vegetables from the pan with a slotted spoon and set aside on a plate.

3 Melt the butter in the pan, then add the mushrooms in batches and fry over brisk heat until lightly coloured. Remove each batch with a slotted spoon and mix with the other vegetables. Pour over any pan juices, then add salt and pepper to taste.

4 Mix together the vegetables and tomato sauce. Add the nutmeg to the cheese sauce. Spoon one-third of the tomato sauce mixture over the bottom of a large baking dish. Cover with one-third of the cheese sauce, then arrange half of the pasta on top.

5 Repeat the layers of tomato, cheese sauce and pasta, then top with the remaining tomato sauce followed by the remaining cheese sauce.

6 Sprinkle the Parmesan cheese evenly over the surface of the lasagne, then bake in the oven at 180°C (350°F) mark 4 for 45 minutes until golden and bubbling. Serve hot, straight from the dish.

Menu Suggestion

Vegetable Lasagne makes a very substantial dish for vegetarians and meat eaters alike. Serve with a simple green salad tossed in a sharp vinaigrette dressing. If you are entertaining friends, a full-bodied red wine such as an Italian Valpolicella or Chianti would hold its own against the strong flavour of the lasagne.

VEGETABLE LASAGNE

Look for the boxes of Italian lasagne with the label 'no pre-cooking required', which are available at most large super-markets. This type of lasagne will save you both time and energy, because it can be layered in the dish straight from the packet. Ordinary lasagne has to be boiled, then drained before using, and it invariably sticks and tears during this process. When using lasagne straight from the packet, always be sure to use plenty of sauce between the layers, as in this recipe, or the finished dish may be dry—this is important if you intend freezing the dish before baking.

BROCCOLI GOUGÈRES

| 1.00 | 🍳 | £ | 378 cals |

Serves 4

700 g (1½ lb) broccoli
25 g (1 oz) butter or margarine
25 g (1 oz) plain flour
300 ml (½ pint) milk
30 ml (2 tbsp) chopped fresh
  parsley
salt and freshly ground pepper
2 egg quantity Choux Pastry
  (page 157)

1 Cut the broccoli into small florets. Cook in boiling salted water for about 10 minutes until nearly tender. Drain well.

2 Melt the butter in a saucepan, add the flour and cook gently, stirring, for 1–2 minutes. Remove from the heat and gradually blend in the milk. Bring to the boil, stirring constantly, then simmer for 3 minutes. Stir in the parsley, with salt and pepper to taste and remove from the heat. Fold in the broccoli florets.

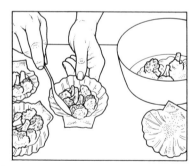

3 Divide the mixture equally between 4 scallop shells or shallow ovenproof dishes, mounding it up slightly in the centre.

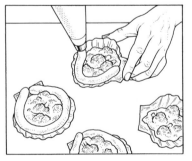

4 Pipe or spoon the choux mixture around the edge of the shells or dishes. Bake in the oven at 200°C (400°F) mark 6 for 35–40 minutes or until well risen and brown. Serve immediately.

Menu Suggestion
Serve these rich individual gougères for a midweek supper dish. Follow with a crisp salad of curly endive and radicchio tossed in a dressing of olive oil, lemon juice and chopped fresh herbs.

BROCCOLI GOUGÈRES
The original gougère came from Burgundy in France; it was a savoury choux pie flavoured with cheese. Nowadays, the term gougère is used to describe any savoury mixture which is encased in a ring of choux pastry, like in this recipe.

LEEK AND CHEESE PIE

1.15 f ✳* 735 cals

*Freeze at step 8, before brushing with beaten egg

Serves 4

3 large leeks, total weight about 450 g (1 lb), trimmed

6 spring onions

40 g (1½ oz) butter or margarine

1 egg

1 egg yolk

30 ml (2 tbsp) double cream

175 g (6 oz) Gruyère cheese, grated

pinch of cayenne

freshly grated nutmeg

salt and freshly ground pepper

225 g (8 oz) Shortcrust Pastry (page 156)

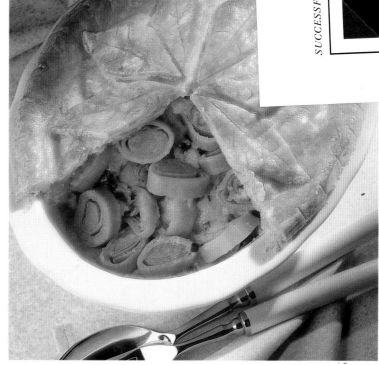

1 Cut the leeks into 1 cm (½ inch) slices, then rinse well under cold running water to remove any grit. Trim the spring onions and chop finely.

2 Melt the butter in a large frying pan and, when foaming, add the leeks. Cook over moderate heat for 5–7 minutes, stirring occasionally, then add the spring onions. Cook for a further 2 minutes, or until the leeks and spring onions are soft but not coloured. Remove from the heat and allow to cool for 5 minutes.

3 Mix the egg, egg yolk, cream and cheese in a bowl. Stir in the leek mixture and add the cayenne with nutmeg, salt and pepper to taste.

4 Cut the pastry into 2 pieces, 1 slightly larger than the other. Shape the larger piece into a ball and roll out until it is 3 mm (⅛ inch) thick and 2.5 cm (1 inch) wider than the top of a 20.5 cm (8 inch) pie dish.

5 Lift the pastry in to the pie dish, taking care not to stretch it. Ease it into place by pressing it with your fingertips, working out-wards from the centre. Ease the pastry carefully up the sides.

6 Spoon the leek and cheese filling into the lined dish, mounding the mixture slightly up towards the centre.

7 Roll out the remaining pastry for the lid until it is 1 cm (½ inch) larger than the circumference of the dish. Brush the pastry rim with water, then lift the lid into position and seal.

8 Trim the edge of the pie, knock up and crimp. Use the pastry trimmings to decorate the top and brush with the beaten egg. Make a slash in the centre of the pie to allow steam to escape.

9 Bake in the oven at 200°C (400°F) mark 6 for about 30 minutes or until golden brown. Allow to cool for about 30 minutes before serving. Serve either warm or cold.

Menu Suggestion
Leek and Cheese Pie is a substantial main course. Serve with a colourful mixed salad to refresh the palate.

BRUSSELS SPROUT SOUFFLÉ

| 1.20 | 🗋 | 295 cals |

Serves 4

butter, for greasing

700 g (1½ lb) Brussels sprouts, trimmed weight

salt and freshly ground pepper

50 g (2 oz) butter or margarine

40 g (1½ oz) plain flour

300 ml (½ pint) milk

pinch of freshly grated nutmeg

3 eggs, separated

1 Butter a 1.3 litre (2¼ pint) soufflé dish. Preheat the oven to 200°C (400°F) mark 6.

2 Cook the Brussels sprouts in boiling salted water for 10–15 minutes until tender. Drain well.

3 Melt the butter in a saucepan, add the flour and cook gently, stirring, for 1–2 minutes. Remove from the heat and gradually blend in the milk. Bring to the boil, stirring constantly, then simmer for 3 minutes until thick and smooth. Add the nutmeg and remove from the heat.

4 Chop half of the sprouts. Work the remaining sprouts in a blender or food processor to a purée with the egg yolks and a little of the sauce. Fold into the rest of the sauce with the chopped sprouts. Season well.

5 Whisk the egg whites until stiff. Gently fold into the Brussels sprout mixture. Turn into the soufflé dish.

6 Bake in the preheated oven for 30–35 minutes until risen. Serve immediately.

Menu Suggestion
Serve for a light lunch or early evening supper followed by a crunchy salad of grated raw vegetables tossed in a yogurt or mayonnaise dressing.

TORTILLA ESPAGNOLA
(SPANISH OMELETTE)

| 1.00 | ☐ | £ | 376 cals |

Serves 4

500 ml (17½ fl oz) vegetable or olive
  oil, for frying

150 g (5 oz) Spanish onion, skinned
  and thinly sliced

salt and freshly ground pepper

4 medium potatoes, about 500 g
  (1 lb) total weight, peeled

4 eggs, size 2

1 Heat 60 ml (4 tbsp) of the oil
in a large, heavy-based frying
pan or omelette pan. Add the
sliced onion and a pinch of salt
and fry gently, stirring frequently
for 10–15 minutes until soft and a
light golden brown. Remove with
a slotted spoon and drain on
absorbent kitchen paper.

2 Cut the potatoes into small
wedges. Dry well with a clean
tea-towel. Pour the remaining oil
into a deep-fat frier and heat to
190°C (375°F). Fry the potatoes in
batches for 5 minutes in the hot
oil, covering the pan so that they
become soft. Remove with a
slotted spoon, place on absorbent
kitchen paper, sprinkle with salt
and leave to drain.

3 Beat the eggs lightly in a
large bowl with salt and
pepper to taste. Stir in the onion
and potatoes.

4 Reheat the oil remaining in the
frying pan until smoking. Pour
all but 30 ml (2 tbsp) of the egg
and potato mixture into the frying
pan. Turn the heat down to low
and let the mixture run to the
sides. Cook for 3–5 minutes until
the underneath is just set.

5 Turn the omelette out upside
down on to a plate. Heat 15 ml
(1 tbsp) of the deep-frying oil in
the frying pan.

6 Pour the reserved egg mixture
into the pan and tip and tilt
the pan so that the egg covers the
base and forms a protective layer
on which to finish cooking the
omelette.

7 Immediately slide in the
omelette, set side uppermost.
Make the edges neat with a palette
knife or spatula and fry for 3–5
minutes until set underneath.
Slide on to a serving plate and
cut into wedges to serve.

Menu Suggestion
Tortilla Espagnola can be served
hot or cold as a main course with a
tomato or green salad. It is also
delicious cold as an appetiser with
drinks before a meal, in which case
it should be sliced into thin
fingers.

PIPÉRADE
(MEDITERRANEAN VEGETABLES WITH EGGS)

| 0.35 | £ ✳* | 334 cals |

* freeze at the end of step 2, without
the eggs and toast

Serves 4

3 large ripe tomatoes

30 ml (2 tbsp) olive or vegetable oil

1 red pepper, cored, seeded and
    chopped

1 small onion, skinned and
    chopped

2 garlic cloves, skinned and
    crushed

salt and freshly ground pepper

50 g (2 oz) butter or margarine,
    softened

4 slices of crusty bread

3 eggs, beaten

chopped fresh parsley, to garnish

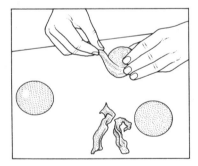

1 Skin the tomatoes. Plunge
them into boiling water for 10
seconds, then into cold. Slip off
the skins with your fingers,
remove the pips and chop the
tomato flesh roughly.

2 Heat 15 ml (1 tbsp) of the olive
oil in a frying pan, add the
tomatoes, red pepper, onion, half
of the garlic and salt and pepper to
taste and fry gently for about 15
minutes, until the vegetables are
soft and pulpy.

3 Meanwhile, cream together
the butter and the remaining
garlic, spread on both sides of the
bread and grill or fry until golden
brown. Keep warm.

4 Add the remaining oil and the
eggs to the vegetables in the
pan and stir gently until the eggs
begin to scramble. Serve at once
with the hot toast, garnished with
plenty of chopped fresh parsley.

Menu Suggestion
In the French Mediterranean,
Pipérade is usually served for a
light evening meal followed by a
green salad tossed in Vinaigrette
dressing (page 151).

ONION SOUFFLÉ QUICHE

| 1.40 | 🍴 | 446–892 cals |

Serves 2–4

175 g (6 oz) Wholemeal Shortcrust
   Pastry (page 157)

2 medium onions, skinned and
   thinly sliced

300 ml (½ pint) milk

1 bay leaf

1 clove

25 g (1 oz) butter or margarine

25 g (1 oz) plain flour

2 eggs, separated

salt and freshly ground pepper

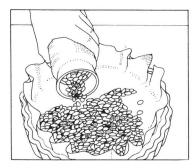

1 Roll out the pastry and use to line a 20.5 cm (8 inch) quiche tin or flan dish. Prick the base with a fork, then line with foil and baking beans.

2 Bake 'blind' in the oven at 200°C (400°F) mark 6 for 15 minutes. Remove the foil and baking beans and bake for a further 5 minutes.

3 Put the onions in a saucepan with the milk, bay leaf and clove. Cover and simmer gently for about 25 minutes or until the onion is quite tender. Discard the bay leaf and clove.

4 Melt the butter in a saucepan, add the flour and cook gently, stirring, for 1–2 minutes. Remove from the heat and gradually blend in the onion and milk mixture. Bring to the boil, stirring constantly, then simmer for 3 minutes until thick and smooth. Remove from the heat and beat in the egg yolks with salt and pepper to taste.

5 Whisk the egg whites until stiff but not dry. Gently fold into the onion mixture. Spoon into the pastry case.

6 Bake the quiche in the oven at 220°C (425°F) mark 7 for 30–35 minutes or until just set. Serve immediately.

Menu Suggestion
Serve for lunch or supper, with a colourful salad such as Chilli Aubergine and Red Pepper Salad (page 81) or Greek Salad (page 87).

ONION SOUFFLÉ QUICHE

Baking a pastry case blind for a quiche may seem time-consuming, but it is well worth the extra effort involved to ensure a crisp pastry crust underneath; a wet filling such as this one would cause the pastry base to become soggy during baking. As an extra precaution, brush a little unwhisked egg white over the pastry after removing the foil and beans in step 2. This acts as a seal and prevents the filling seeping into the pastry and making it soft.

STUFFED AUBERGINES

| 1.30 | £ | 524 cals |

Serves 4

2 medium aubergines

salt and freshly ground pepper

75 ml (5 tbsp) olive oil

1 medium onion, skinned and finely chopped

1–2 garlic cloves, skinned and crushed

1 red or green pepper, cored, seeded and finely diced

175 g (6 oz) button mushrooms, wiped and finely chopped

4 ripe tomatoes, skinned and finely chopped

15 ml (1 tbsp) tomato purée

100 g (4 oz) long grain rice

50 g (2 oz) chopped mixed nuts

30 ml (2 tbsp) chopped fresh parsley

100 g (4 oz) Cheddar cheese, grated

75 g (3 oz) fresh wholemeal breadcrumbs

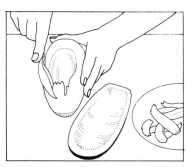

1 Slice the aubergines in half lengthways. Scoop out and reserve the flesh, leaving a narrow margin inside the skin so that the aubergines will hold their shape.

2 Sprinkle the insides of the aubergine shells with salt and stand upside down to drain for 30 minutes.

3 Dice the scooped-out aubergine flesh, then place in a colander, sprinkling each layer with salt. Cover with a plate, place heavy weights on top and leave to dégorge for 30 minutes.

4 Meanwhile, heat 60 ml (4 tbsp) of the oil in a heavy-based saucepan. Add the onion and garlic; fry gently for 5 minutes until soft. Add the diced pepper to the pan and fry gently for 5 minutes.

5 Rinse the diced aubergine under cold running water, then pat dry with absorbent kitchen paper. Add to the pan with the mushrooms, tomatoes and tomato purée. Simmer for about 5 minutes, then add the rice, nuts, parsley and salt and pepper.

6 Rinse the aubergine cases and pat dry with absorbent kitchen paper. Brush a baking dish with the remaining oil, then stand the aubergine cases in the dish. Fill with the stuffing mixture.

7 Mix the grated cheese and breadcrumbs together, then sprinkle evenly over the top of the aubergines. Bake uncovered in the oven at 180°C (350°F) mark 4 for 45 minutes. Serve hot.

Menu Suggestion

Aubergines stuffed with rice and vegetables make a most nutritious main course dish for a family supper or an informal party. Serve with extra boiled rice, and Tomato Sauce (page 149).

AVIYAL
(MIXED VEGETABLE CURRY)

| 1.00 | £ | ✳* | 252–378 cals |

* freeze before garnishing at the
end of step 5

Serves 4–6

60 ml (4 tbsp) ghee or vegetable oil

2 onions, skinned and thinly sliced

1 garlic clove, skinned and
  crushed

1 cooking apple, peeled, cored and
  roughly chopped

2.5 cm (1 inch) piece of fresh root
  ginger, peeled and roughly
  chopped

15 ml (1 tbsp) mustard seeds

10 ml (2 tsp) coriander seeds

10 ml (2 tsp) cumin seeds

5 ml (1 tsp) turmeric

2.5–5 ml ($\frac{1}{2}$–1 tsp) chilli powder

225 g (8 oz) tomatoes, skinned and
  roughly chopped

salt and freshly ground pepper

350 g (12 oz) potatoes, peeled and
  diced

225 g (8 oz) carrots, peeled and
  diced

225 g (8 oz) cauliflower florets

225 g (8 oz) fresh or frozen French
  beans or peas

50 g (2 oz) chopped mixed nuts

30 ml (2 tbsp) desiccated coconut

1 Heat half of the ghee in a
heavy-based large saucepan or
flameproof casserole. Add the
onions, garlic, apple and ginger
and fry gently for about 10
minutes, stirring occasionally,
until soft and lightly coloured.

2 Meanwhile, put the mustard,
coriander and cumin seeds in a
small, heavy-based frying pan and
dry-fry for 2–3 minutes, shaking
the pan and stirring the spices
frequently.

3 Turn the spices into a mortar
and crush finely with a pestle
(or work in a nut mill). Add the
crushed spices to the onion
mixture, with the turmeric and
chilli powder. Fry gently, stirring,
for 2–3 minutes, then add the
tomatoes. Stir well to mix, breaking up the tomatoes with a wooden
spoon. Add salt and pepper.

4 Add the potatoes and carrots
to the pan, then pour in 600 ml
(1 pint) water. Bring to the boil,
stirring, then lower the heat, cover
and simmer for 15 minutes.

5 Separate the cauliflower
florets into small sprigs. Add
to the pan with the beans or peas
and cook until vegetables are
tender. (This should take 10–15
minutes, depending on whether
beans or peas are fresh or frozen.)

6 Before serving, heat the
remaining ghee in the frying
pan. Add the nuts and coconut
and fry over moderate heat,
shaking the pan constantly.

7 Taste and adjust the seasoning
of the vegetables, then turn
into a warmed serving dish.
Sprinkle with the nut and coconut
mixture and serve immediately.

Menu Suggestion
Serve for a family meal with
brown rice or a nutty pilaf, and a
yogurt and cucumber salad. A
dish of curried lentils (dal) would
make the meal most nutritious.

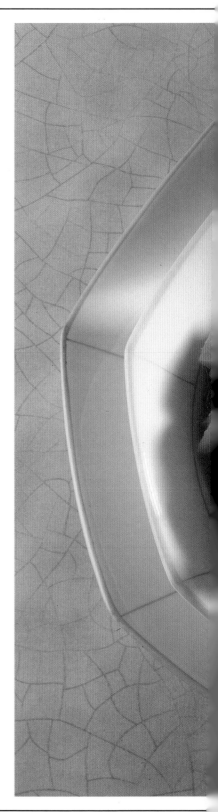

ZUCCHINI ALLA PARMIGIANA
(ITALIAN COURGETTE, PARMESAN AND TOMATO BAKE)

| 1.00 | £ | ✳ | 517 cals |

Serves 4

700 g (1½ lb) courgettes

salt and freshly ground pepper

about 150 ml (¼ pint) vegetable oil

1 medium onion, skinned and finely chopped

450 g (1 lb) tomatoes, skinned and chopped

1 large garlic clove, skinned and crushed

30 ml (2 tbsp) tomato purée

15 ml (1 tbsp) chopped fresh marjoram or 5 ml (1 tsp) dried

two 170 g (6 oz) packets Mozzarella cheese, thinly sliced

75 g (3 oz) freshly grated Parmesan cheese

1 Cut the courgettes into 0.5 cm (¼ inch) thick slices. Sprinkle with salt and leave to dégorge for at least 20 minutes.

2 Heat 30 ml (2 tbsp) of the oil in a saucepan, add the onion and fry for about 5 minutes until just beginning to brown.

3 Stir in the tomatoes, garlic, tomato purée and salt and pepper. Simmer for about 10 minutes, stirring with a wooden spoon to break down the tomatoes. Stir in the marjoram and remove from the heat.

4 Rinse the courgettes and pat dry with absorbent kitchen paper. Heat half of the remaining oil in a frying pan, add half of the courgettes and fry until golden brown. Drain well on kitchen paper while frying the remaining courgettes in the remaining oil.

5 Layer the courgettes, tomato sauce and Mozzarella cheese in a shallow ovenproof dish, finishing with a layer of Mozzarella. Sprinkle with the Parmesan cheese.

6 Bake in the oven at 180°C (350°F) mark 4 for about 40 minutes or until brown and bubbling. Serve hot, straight from the dish.

Menu Suggestion
This makes a rich and filling main course served with crusty French bread and a mixed side salad such as Radicchio and Alfalfa Salad (page 67).

Jerusalem Artichoke Gratin

| 1.20 | £ | ✳* | 725 cals |

* freeze before baking at end of step 10

Serves 4

900 g (2 lb) Jerusalem artichokes

salt and freshly ground black pepper

225 g (8 oz) small button or pickling onions

3 medium leeks, trimmed

75 g (3 oz) butter or margarine

15 ml (1 tbsp) olive oil

2 garlic cloves, skinned and crushed

150 ml ($\frac{1}{4}$ pint) dry white wine or vegetable stock, or a mixture of both

1.25 ml ($\frac{1}{4}$ tsp) freshly grated nutmeg

225 g (8 oz) fresh or frozen peas

150 ml ($\frac{1}{4}$ pint) double cream

75 g (3 oz) Gruyère cheese, grated

75 g (3 oz) Cheddar cheese, grated

50 g (2 oz) dried wholemeal breadcrumbs

1 Parboil the Jerusalem artichokes in salted water for 10 minutes. Remove with a slotted spoon and leave until cool enough to handle.

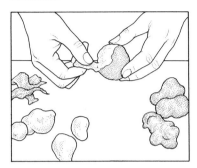

2 Peel the skins off the Jerusalem artichokes and slice the flesh thickly. Set aside.

3 Add the button onions to the water and boil for 2 minutes, then remove with a slotted spoon. Peel off the skins, leaving the root ends intact so that the onions remain whole.

4 Slice the leeks thickly, then wash well under cold running water to remove any grit.

5 Heat 50 g (2 oz) of the butter with the oil in a heavy-based saucepan, add the onions and garlic and toss over moderate heat until the onions are well coated in the butter and oil.

6 Pour in the wine and 150 ml ($\frac{1}{4}$ pint) water and bring to the boil. Add the nutmeg, cover and simmer for 10 minutes.

7 Add the artichokes, leeks and peas and continue simmering for 5 minutes or until all the vegetables are tender. With a slotted spoon, transfer vegetables to a flameproof gratin dish.

8 Boil the cooking liquid rapidly until reduced to about half of its original volume. Lower the heat and stir in the cream.

9 Mix the 2 cheeses together. Stir half of this mixture into the sauce. Add salt and pepper to taste and stir until the cheeses have melted.

10 Pour the cheese sauce over the vegetables in the dish. Mix the remaining cheese with the breadcrumbs, then sprinkle evenly over the top.

11 Dot the remaining butter over the gratin, then bake in the oven at 220°C (425°F) mark 7 for 10 minutes, until the topping is golden brown. Serve hot, straight from the dish.

Menu Suggestion
Served with chunky slices of granary or wholemeal bread, this vegetable gratin makes a tasty and nutritious main dish for a family lunch or supper.

VEGETABLE KEBABS WITH TOFU SAUCE

| 0.40 | £ | 482 cals |

Serves 2

297 g (10½ oz) carton silken tofu

30 ml (2 tbsp) olive or vegetable oil

20 ml (4 tsp) soy sauce

about 30 ml (2 tbsp) lemon juice

1–2 garlic cloves, skinned and crushed

15 ml (1 tbsp) sesame oil (optional)

salt and freshly ground pepper

4 small courgettes

6 pieces of baby sweetcorn, halved crossways

16 button mushrooms, wiped

12 cherry tomatoes, or 3 medium tomatoes, quartered

12 bay leaves

30 ml (2 tbsp) sesame seeds

1 First prepare the tofu sauce. Put the tofu in a blender or food processor with half of the oil and soy sauce, the lemon juice, garlic and sesame oil (if using). Work until the ingredients are evenly combined, then add salt and pepper to taste and more lemon juice, if liked. Pour into a jug and chill in the refrigerator while making the kebabs.

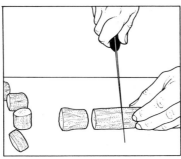

2 Trim the ends off the courgettes, then cut each courgette into 3 chunky pieces. Blanch in boiling salted water for 1 minute only, then drain.

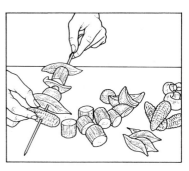

3 Thread the vegetables and bay leaves on to 4 oiled kebab skewers, alternating the different ingredients as much as possible.

4 Place the kebabs on the rack of the grill pan. Mix the remaining oil and soy sauce with the sesame seeds. Brush over the kebabs. Cook under a preheated grill for about 10 minutes, turning frequently and brushing with more of the oil and soy sauce mixture.

5 Serve the vegetable kebabs hot, with the chilled tofu sauce handed separately in a jug or sauceboat.

Menu Suggestion

For a nutritious main course, arrange these tasty kebabs on a bed of brown rice. Serve a crisp mixed salad separately. On their own, the kebabs also make a good starter for a vegetarian meal, in which case they will serve 4 people.

VEGETABLE KEBABS WITH TOFU SAUCE

Silken tofu is available from chilling cabinets in health food shops. It is a kind of bean curd made from soya beans, used extensively in oriental cooking for its nutritive value. Weight for weight it contains as much protein as meat, yet it is very low in fat, and much cheaper.

CABBAGE AND HAZELNUT CROQUETTES

| 1.00* | 🍳 | £ | ❄ | 141 cals |

* plus 2 hours chilling

Makes 16

450 g (1 lb) potatoes, peeled

salt and freshly ground pepper

900 g (2 lb) cabbage, roughly chopped

45 ml (3 tbsp) milk

50 g (2 oz) butter or margarine

50 g (2 oz) plain flour

50 g (2 oz) hazelnuts, chopped and toasted

2 eggs, beaten

100 g (4 oz) dry white breadcrumbs

vegetable oil, for deep frying

lemon wedges, to serve

1 Boil the potatoes in salted water for about 20 minutes until tender. Drain them well and mash without adding any liquid.

2 Cook the cabbage in boiling salted water for 5–10 minutes or until just tender. Drain well. Purée in a blender or food processor, adding the milk if required—you should have 450 ml (¾ pint) purée.

3 Melt the butter in a saucepan, add the flour and cook gently, stirring, for 1–2 minutes. Gradually blend in the cabbage purée and milk. Bring to the boil, then simmer for 5 minutes.

4 Stir the mashed potatoes and hazelnuts into the sauce, add salt and pepper to taste and mix well. Transfer to a bowl, cool, cover and chill in the refrigerator for at least 1½ hours or until firm.

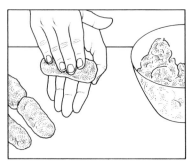

5 With dampened hands, shape the mixture into 16 croquettes. Place on a greased baking sheet and chill again for at least 20 minutes.

6 Coat the croquettes in the beaten eggs and breadcrumbs. Heat the oil to 180°C (350°F) in a deep-fat frier. Deep fry the croquettes in batches for about 4 minutes until crisp and golden. Remove with a slotted spoon and drain on absorbent kitchen paper while frying the remainder. Serve hot, with lemon wedges.

Menu Suggestion

These nutty croquettes taste good with a crunchy salad such as Crisp Endive with Orange and Croûtons (page 64). They would also go well with Beetroot Salad with Mint (page 84).

CABBAGE AND HAZELNUT CROQUETTES

Hazelnuts get their name from the Anglo-Saxon word 'haesil', meaning head-dress. This is an apt description, for the outer covering fits over the nut itself. Other names for hazelnuts are filberts and cob nuts, depending on the part of the world in which they are grown. These three nuts are not exactly the same, but they are all close relations of the Corylus family, and are interchangeable in recipes.

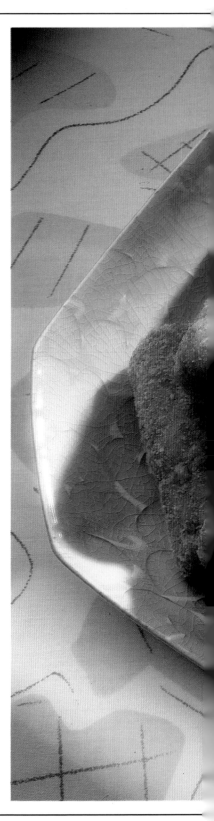

SWISS STUFFED POTATOES

1.30	£	346 cals

Serves 4

4 medium baking potatoes

50 g (2 oz) butter or margarine

1 small onion, skinned and finely chopped

450 g (1 lb) fresh spinach, cooked, drained and chopped, or 225 g (8 oz) frozen chopped spinach

100 g (4 oz) full fat soft cheese

1.25 ml ($\frac{1}{4}$ tsp) freshly grated nutmeg

salt and freshly ground pepper

50 g (2 oz) Gruyère or Emmental cheese, grated

pinch of paprika or cayenne

1 Scrub the potatoes under cold running water, then pat dry with absorbent kitchen paper.

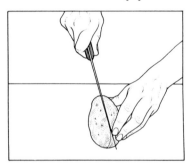

2 With a sharp, pointed knife, score a line in the skin around the middle of each potato.

3 Place the potatoes directly on the oven shelf and bake at 200°C (400°F) mark 6 for 1$\frac{1}{4}$ hours or until tender.

4 About 15 minutes before the end of the cooking time, melt the butter in a heavy-based saucepan, add the onion and fry gently for about 5 minutes until soft and lightly coloured. Add the fresh spinach and cook gently for 2–3 minutes, stirring frequently. (If using frozen spinach, cook for 7–10 minutes until thawed.) Remove from the heat.

5 When the potatoes are cooked, slice in half lengthways. Scoop out the flesh into a bowl and add the spinach mixture, the soft cheese, nutmeg and salt and pepper to taste. Mix well.

6 Spoon the mixture into the potato shells, mounding it up in the centre. Stand the stuffed potatoes on a baking sheet. Sprinkle over the cheese and finally the paprika or cayenne. Return to the oven for 10–15 minutes, until the cheese topping is bubbling and golden. Serve hot.

Menu Suggestion
These stuffed baked potatoes are very filling. Serve them on their own for a hearty lunch or supper, followed by a crisp and colourful salad such as Radicchio and Alfalfa Salad (page 67).

Mexican Baked Potatoes

| 1.25 | £ | 367 cals |

Serves 4

4 medium baking potatoes

30 ml (2 tbsp) vegetable oil

1 medium onion, skinned and finely chopped

1 garlic clove, skinned and crushed

397 g (14 oz) can tomatoes

10 ml (2 tsp) tomato purée

2.5 ml ($\frac{1}{2}$ tsp) chilli powder

pinch of granulated sugar

salt and freshly ground pepper

432 g (15.25 oz) can red kidney beans, drained

30 ml (2 tbsp) chopped fresh parsley

50 g (2 oz) mature or farmhouse Cheddar cheese, coarsely grated

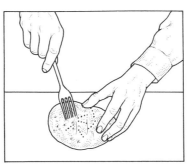

1 Scrub the potatoes under cold running water, then pat dry. Brush with a little vegetable oil, prick all over with a skewer or fork. Bake at 200°C (400°F) mark 6 for 1¼ hours or until tender.

2 Meanwhile, make the stuffing. Heat the remaining oil in a saucepan, add the onion and garlic and fry gently until soft.

3 Add tomatoes with their juice and stir to break up with a wooden spoon. Add the tomato purée, chilli powder, sugar and salt and pepper to taste and bring to the boil, stirring. Simmer, uncovered, for about 20 minutes, stirring occasionally. Add beans and parsley and heat through.

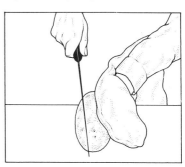

4 When the potatoes are cooked, slice off the top third of each one and reserve for lids. Scoop out some of the potato from the bottom third of each one and add to the tomato sauce.

5 Place 1 potato on each serving plate and spoon the chilli bean mixture into each one, letting it spill out on to the plate. Sprinkle grated cheese on top, then replace the lids at an angle. Serve immediately.

Menu Suggestion
This vegetarian dish is hot, spicy and substantial. Serve for a hearty supper, accompanied by a crisp green salad and glasses of chilled beer or lager.

JACKET BAKED POTATOES

The best potatoes to use for baking are Maris Piper, Desirée and Pentland Squire, although King Edward and Pentland Crown are almost as good. Slightly different methods of baking are used in these 2 recipes. Scoring a line around the middle before baking, as in Swiss Stuffed Potatoes (facing page), makes them easier to cut for stuffing; brushing them with oil, as in Mexican Baked Potatoes (above), gives a crisper skin.

Salads and Cold Dishes

Choose from exotic salads with beansprouts and okra, continental salads with radicchio and endive, Middle Eastern stuffed vegetables, and unusual combinations of vegetables and fruit, and forget those days when a salad meant little more than lettuce, tomato and cucumber!

ORIENTAL SALAD

| 0.20 | £ | 112 cals |

Serves 8

1 large cucumber
salt and freshly ground pepper
1 small head Chinese leaves
1 red pepper
125 g (4 oz) button mushrooms
225 g (8 oz) beansprouts
30 ml (2 tbsp) soy sauce
15 ml (1 tbsp) peanut butter
30 ml (2 tbsp) sesame oil
30 ml (2 tbsp) rice or wine vinegar
50 g (2 oz) shelled unsalted peanuts

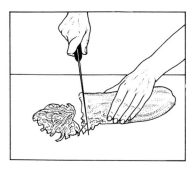

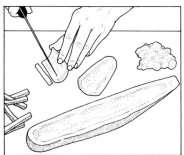

1 Cut the cucumber in half lengthways and scoop out the seeds. Cut the halves into 5 cm (2 inch) sticks, leaving the skin on.

2 Shred the Chinese leaves, wash and drain well. Cut the red pepper in half and remove the core and seeds. Cut the flesh into thin strips. Wipe and slice the mushrooms. Rinse the beansprouts and drain well.

3 Just before serving, mix the soy sauce in a large bowl with the peanut butter, oil, vinegar and salt and pepper to taste. Add the salad ingredients and the peanuts and toss together. Transfer to a serving bowl.

Menu Suggestion

Serve the salad in pockets of pitta bread as an accompaniment to barbecued food or at a picnic.

ORIENTAL SALAD

All the exotic ingredients for this salad can be bought in good supermarkets or health food shops. *Chinese leaves* are an extremely versatile vegetable and can be lightly braised, steamed or served raw in salads. Look for Chinese leaves also under the name of Chinese cabbage or Chinese celery cabbage; it has long white stems and should not be confused with a similar-looking vegetable called 'bok choy', which has dark green stems. *Beansprouts* are the shoots of sprouted mung peas or beans. They are available fresh, and should be eaten as soon as possible after purchase as they quickly discolour and become limp. *Soy sauce* comes in varying strengths, from light to dark brown. For a salad, dark soy sauce is the best one to use because it is fairly mild; light soy sauce can be very salty. *Sesame oil* is made from sesame seeds. It has a rich, golden-brown colour and a nutty aroma and flavour. In Chinese cooking, it is used as a seasoning rather than for cooking, because it burns quickly when heated. *Rice wine vinegar* is available in white, red and black varieties. Each one has a slightly different flavour, from sweet and spicy to rich and pungent. They are cheap, so it is a good idea to try different makes to find which you like best.

CRISP ENDIVE WITH ORANGE AND CROÛTONS

| 0.20 | £ | 138 cals |

Serves 8

| 1 large head of curly endive |
| ½ bunch of watercress |
| 2 large oranges |
| 2 thick slices of white bread |
| vegetable oil, for shallow frying |
| 60 ml (4 tbsp) olive oil |
| 60 ml (4 tbsp) white wine vinegar |
| 2.5 ml (½ tsp) caster sugar |
| salt and freshly ground pepper |

1 Remove and discard any coarse or discoloured leaves from the endive. Tear the endive into pieces, wash and dry thoroughly with a clean tea towel. Wash, trim and dry the watercress.

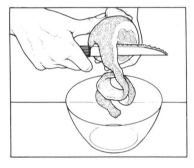

2 With a small serrated knife and working over a bowl to catch the juices, cut away all the skin and pith from the oranges. Reserve the juices.

3 Cut the orange flesh into segments, leaving the membrane behind. Remove any pips with the tip of the knife.

4 Arrange the endive, watercress and orange in a serving bowl. Cut the crusts off the bread and cut the bread into 1 cm (½ inch) cubes. Heat the vegetable oil in a frying pan, add the cubes of bread and fry until crisp and golden. Remove the croûtons with a slotted spoon and drain well on absorbent kitchen paper. Sprinkle with salt.

5 In a jug, whisk the reserved orange juice with the olive oil, vinegar, sugar and salt and pepper to taste. Pour over the salad and add the croûtons just before serving.

Menu Suggestion
This colourful winter salad is good with rich meat dishes, especially duck and game.

CRISP ENDIVE WITH ORANGE AND CROÛTONS

Although native to the Mediterranean, curly endive is now grown in other temperate countries throughout the world, and is available virtually all year round. At its best, curly endive is crisp, pale green and frondy, with a mildly bitter flavour. It does not keep well and quickly goes limp and yellow. Most heads of endive are very large, but some greengrocers will split them in halves or quarters. Take care not to confuse curly endive with the torpedo-shaped chicory. In France, chicory is called endive, whereas curly endive is called *chicorée frisée* or 'frizzy chicory'.

TOMATO AND OKRA VINAIGRETTE

| 0.15 | £ | 191 cals |

Serves 8

450 g (1 lb) okra
150 ml (¼ pint) vegetable oil
30 ml (2 tbsp) lemon juice
5 ml (1 tsp) tomato purée
pinch of caster sugar
salt and freshly ground pepper
450 g (1 lb) tomatoes, skinned

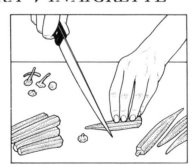

1 Trim off the tops and tails of the okra. Cook in boiling salted water for about 4 minutes or until just tender. Drain well and place in a bowl.

2 In a jug, whisk together the oil, lemon juice, tomato purée, sugar, and salt and pepper to taste. Pour over the warm okra and fold gently to mix.

3 Slice the tomatoes thinly. Arrange in a serving bowl with the okra and vinaigrette. Cover and chill in the refrigerator for at least 30 minutes before serving.

Menu Suggestion
Serve for an unusual and attractive first course, with hot garlic or herb bread. Or serve as a side salad — okra goes particularly well with lamb.

RADICCHIO AND ALFALFA SALAD

0.15	£	141–212 cals

Serves 4–6

2 heads of radicchio

50–75 g (2–3 oz) alfalfa sprouts

90 ml (6 tbsp) olive or vegetable oil

30 ml (2 tbsp) white wine vinegar

15 ml (1 tbsp) single cream
  (optional)

1 small garlic clove, skinned and
  crushed

1.25 ml ($\frac{1}{4}$ tsp) granulated sugar

salt and freshly ground pepper

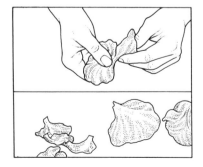

1 Tear the radicchio into bite-sized pieces. Wash, drain and pat dry on absorbent kitchen paper. Wash and dry the alfalfa sprouts.

2 Mix the alfalfa and radicchio together in a serving bowl. In a jug, whisk together the remaining ingredients, with salt and pepper to taste. Just before serving, pour over the radicchio and alfalfa and toss together.

Menu Suggestion

Serve as a side salad whenever a colourful and crunchy accompaniment is required, or serve with a selection of cheeses and wholemeal or granary bread for a nutritious lunch.

SALAD ELONA

| 0.40 | £ | 108 cals |

Serves 4

½ medium cucumber

salt

225 g (8 oz) fresh ripe strawberries

10 ml (2 tsp) green peppercorns in brine

45 ml (3 tbsp) sunflower or corn oil

15 ml (1 tbsp) vinegar (see box)

a few lettuce leaves, to serve

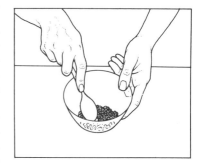

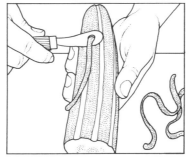

1 Score the skin of the cucumber lengthways with a cannelle knife or the prongs of a fork. Slice the cucumber very thinly, then place on a plate and sprinkle with salt. Leave to stand for about 30 minutes to draw out the excess moisture.

2 Meanwhile, prepare the strawberries. Reserve a few whole fruit (the smallest possible) for the garnish. Hull the remaining strawberries, and slice in half lengthways.

3 Drain the peppercorns and pat dry with absorbent kitchen paper. Crush them with the back of a metal spoon in a small bowl. Add the oil and vinegar and whisk with a fork until well combined.

4 Drain the cucumber and pat dry with absorbent kitchen paper. Shred the lettuce, then arrange on a round serving platter. Arrange the cucumber slices and halved strawberries on the lettuce, alternating rings of each. Sprinkle over the dressing, then garnish the centre with the reserved whole strawberries. Serve as soon as possible.

Menu Suggestion

Sweet and tangy, this cucumber and strawberry side salad is perfect with delicate fish such as salmon and trout. It is also delicious with light or plain poultry dishes, particularly chicken either hot or cold.

SALAD ELONA

The combination of sweet and sour in this salad is unusual, but most refreshing. Do not use malt vinegar as it is too strong. Wine vinegar can be used, but if you are able to get to an Italian delicatessen, buy balsamic vinegar or *aceto balsamico*. This is perfect for serving with fruit, and can also be used in dressings for green salads, and for sprinkling over roast and barbecued meat just before serving.

Balsamic vinegar comes from Modena in northern Italy, where it is made from specially sweet grapes and aged for many years in wooden vats; it is said to have medicinal properties.

Do not make this salad in advance as the strawberries will discolour the cucumber. Serve soon after assembling.

TOMATO, AVOCADO AND PASTA SALAD

| 0.20 | £ | 626 cals |

Serves 4

175 g (6 oz) small wholemeal pasta
   shells

salt and freshly ground pepper

105 ml (7 tbsp) olive oil

45 ml (3 tbsp) lemon juice

5 ml (1 tsp) wholegrain mustard

30 ml (2 tbsp) chopped fresh basil

2 ripe avocados

2 red onions

16 black olives

225 g (8 oz) ripe cherry tomatoes,
   if available, or small salad
   tomatoes

fresh basil leaves, to garnish

1 Cook the pasta in plenty of boiling salted water for about 5 minutes until just tender. Drain in a colander and rinse under cold running water to stop the pasta cooking further. Cool for 20 minutes.

2 Meanwhile, whisk the oil in a bowl with the lemon juice, mustard, chopped basil and salt and pepper to taste.

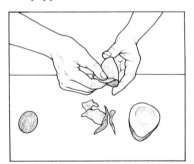

3 Halve and stone the avocados then peel off the skins. Chop the avocado flesh into large pieces and fold gently into the dressing.

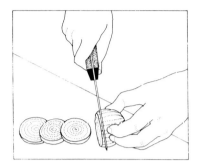

4 Slice the onions thinly into rings. Stone the olives. Halve the tomatoes and mix them with the onion rings, the olives and the cold pasta shells.

5 Spoon the pasta and tomato on to 4 individual serving plates. Spoon over the avocado and dressing and garnish with fresh basil leaves. Serve immediately.

Menu Suggestion
This pretty salad makes a delicious summer starter. Serve with chunky slices of fresh wholemeal bread and butter, with a chilled dry white wine to drink. Alternatively, serve the salad as an accompaniment to barbecued or grilled meat.

RAW SPINACH AND MUSHROOM SALAD

| 0.50 | f | 402–604 cals |

Serves 2–3

225 g (8 oz) young spinach leaves

225 g (8 oz) button mushrooms

2 thick slices of white bread

90 ml (6 tbsp) olive oil

25 g (1 oz) butter or margarine

1 garlic clove, skinned and
   crushed

30 ml (2 tbsp) tarragon vinegar

5 ml (1 tsp) tarragon mustard

salt and freshly ground pepper

1 Wash the spinach well,
discarding any damaged or
yellowing leaves. Cut out and
discard any thick ribs.

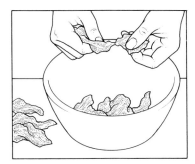

2 Tear the spinach leaves into a
large salad bowl, discarding
any thick stalks.

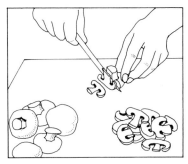

3 Wipe the mushrooms but do
not peel them. Slice them
thinly into neat 'T' shapes.

4 Add the mushrooms to the
spinach. Using your hands,
toss the 2 ingredients together. Set
aside while making the croûtons
and dressing.

5 Cut the crusts off the bread
and cut the bread into 1 cm
($\frac{1}{2}$ inch) cubes. Heat the oil and
butter in a frying pan, add the
garlic and the cubes of bread and
fry until crisp and golden. Remove
the croûtons with a slotted spoon
and drain well on absorbent
kitchen paper.

6 Add the vinegar to the oil in
the pan, with the mustard and
salt and pepper to taste. Stir well
to combine, then remove the pan
from the heat and leave to cool
for 5 minutes.

7 Add the croûtons to the salad,
then the dressing. Toss well
to combine and serve immediately.

Menu Suggestion
This nutritious salad of raw
ingredients tossed in a warm oil
and vinegar dressing makes an
unusual light lunch or supper.
Serve with hot crusty rolls.

AVOCADO AND LEMON SALAD WITH OMELETTE RINGS

| 0.30* | £ | 412–618 cals |

Serves 4–6

4 eggs

50 g (2 oz) Cheddar cheese, grated

salt and freshly ground pepper

25 g (1 oz) butter or margarine

5 ml (1 tsp) whole black peppercorns

5 ml (1 tsp) whole coriander seeds

90 ml (6 tbsp) olive or vegetable oil

45 ml (3 tbsp) lemon juice

2 ripe avocados

parsley sprigs, to garnish (optional)

1 Put the eggs in a bowl with the cheese, 15 ml (1 tbsp) water and salt and pepper to taste. Whisk together.

2 Melt a quarter of the butter in an omelette pan or small non-stick frying pan. When foaming, pour in a quarter of the egg mixture. After a few seconds, push the set egg mixture into the centre of the pan to allow the uncooked egg to run to the edges. Cook until just set.

3 Brown the omelette under a preheated hot grill. Turn out on to a plate. Repeat with the remaining egg mixture to make another 3 omelettes.

4 While the omelettes are still warm, roll them up loosely. Wrap in greaseproof paper and leave to cool.

5 Meanwhile, crush the peppercorns and coriander seeds coarsely with a pestle and mortar, or with the end of a rolling pin in a sturdy bowl.

6 In a bowl, whisk together the oil, lemon juice, crushed spices and salt and pepper to taste. Halve, stone and peel the avocados, then slice thickly into the dressing. Toss gently to coat completely.

7 Slice the omelettes thinly. Arrange the omelette rings and avocado slices on individual serving plates. Spoon over the dressing and garnish with sprigs of parsley, if liked. Serve immediately.

Menu Suggestion
Omelette rings and avocado slices combine together to make this a substantial and nutritious salad. Serve for a main course at lunch-time, with wholemeal French-style bread, or as a light supper.

FENNEL À LA GRECQUE
(GREEK-STYLE MARINATED FENNEL)

| 1.10* | £ | ✳ | 249 cals |

* plus 30 minutes cooling and 1 hour chilling

Serves 4

90 ml (6 tbsp) olive or vegetable oil

1 large onion, skinned and finely chopped

1 garlic clove, skinned and finely chopped

150 ml ($\frac{1}{4}$ pint) dry white wine

4 ripe tomatoes, skinned and chopped

juice of $\frac{1}{2}$ lemon

10 ml (2 tsp) tomato purée

1 bay leaf

5 ml (1 tsp) coriander seeds, crushed

5 ml (1 tsp) granulated sugar

2.5 ml ($\frac{1}{2}$ tsp) chopped fresh basil

salt and freshly ground pepper

2 medium fennel heads

1 Heat the oil in a large sauce-pan, add the onion and garlic and fry gently for about 10 minutes or until they are soft but not coloured.

2 Add the wine, tomatoes, lemon juice, tomato purée, bay leaf, crushed coriander, sugar, basil and salt and pepper to taste. Bring to the boil, stirring, then cover and simmer for 20 minutes.

3 Meanwhile, trim the fennel of any green feathery tops and set aside for the garnish.

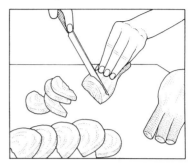

4 Remove and discard any discoloured patches from the fennel, halve the heads and slice them thinly.

5 Bring a large saucepan of salted water to the boil, add the fennel and blanch for 5 minutes. Drain the fennel well, add to the tomato sauce, cover and simmer gently for about 30 minutes.

6 Leave to cool for 30 minutes, then cover with cling film and chill in the refrigerator for at least 1 hour.

7 Before serving, chop the reserved fennel tops finely. Taste and adjust the seasoning of the tomato sauce, then turn into a serving dish and garnish with the chopped fennel. Serve chilled.

Menu Suggestion
The flavour of fennel goes particularly well with lamb and chicken, and the tomato sauce makes this dish most suitable for serving with plain roast or grilled meat. The salad also makes the most delicious first course, served with crusty French bread to mop up the juices.

CELERIAC AND BEAN SALAD

1.10* f	226–339 cals

* plus overnight soaking, 20 minutes
cooling and 1 hour chilling

Serves 4–6

225 g (8 oz) dried flageolet beans,
   soaked in cold water overnight

1 large green pepper

finely grated rind and juice of
   1 lemon

60 ml (4 tbsp) olive or vegetable oil

15 ml (1 tbsp) whole grain mustard

1 garlic clove, skinned and
   crushed

45 ml (3 tbsp) chopped fresh
   parsley

salt and freshly ground pepper

225 g (8 oz) celeriac

1 Drain the soaked beans and
rinse well under cold running
water. Put the beans in a large
saucepan and cover with plenty of
fresh cold water. Bring slowly to
the boil, then skim off any scum
with a slotted spoon. Half cover
the pan with a lid and simmer
gently for about 1 hour, or until
the beans are just tender.

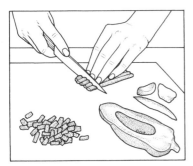

2 Meanwhile, halve the pepper
and remove the core and seeds.
Cut the flesh into strips and then
into cubes.

3 In a bowl, whisk together the
grated lemon rind, about 30 ml
(2 tbsp) lemon juice, the oil,
mustard, garlic, parsley and salt
and pepper to taste.

4 Just before the beans are
ready, peel the celeriac and
chop roughly into 2.5 cm (1 inch)
cubes. Blanch in boiling salted
water for 5 minutes. Drain well.

5 Drain the beans well and place
in a bowl. Add the celeriac
and toss all the salad ingredients
together while the beans and
celeriac are still hot. Leave to cool
for 20 minutes, then cover and
chill in the refrigerator for at least
1 hour before serving. Serve
chilled.

Menu Suggestion
Serve this tangy, nutritious salad
as a first course with hot garlic or
herb bread. It would also make a
good side salad to serve with meat
and poultry dishes.

WINTER CABBAGE AND CAULIFLOWER SALAD

0.25* £ 480 cals

* plus about 1 hour chilling

Serves 4

225 g (8 oz) hard white cabbage

225 g (8 oz) cauliflower florets

2 large carrots, peeled

75 g (3 oz) mixed shelled nuts, roughly chopped

50 g (2 oz) raisins

60 ml (4 tbsp) chopped fresh parsley or coriander

90 ml (6 tbsp) mayonnaise

90 ml (6 tbsp) soured cream or natural yogurt

10 ml (2 tsp) French mustard

30 ml (2 tbsp) olive or vegetable oil

juice of $\frac{1}{2}$ lemon

salt and freshly ground pepper

3 red-skinned eating apples

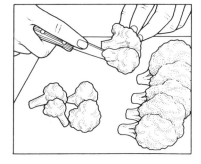

1 Shred the cabbage finely with a sharp knife and place in a large bowl. Divide the cauliflower florets into small sprigs and add to the cabbage. Mix the vegetables gently with your hands.

2 Grate the carrots into the bowl, then add the nuts, raisins and parsley. Mix the vegetables together again until evenly combined.

3 Put the remaining ingredients except the apples in a jug. Whisk well to combine, then pour over the vegetables in the bowl and toss well.

4 Core and chop the apples, but do not peel them. Add to the salad and toss again to combine with the other ingredients. Cover the bowl and chill the salad in the refrigerator for about 1 hour before serving.

Menu Suggestion
This crunchy, colourful salad can be served as an accompaniment to a selection of cold meats for a quick and nutritious lunch. With extra nuts, for vegetarians, it would make a meal in itself, served with cheese and wholemeal or granary bread.

GADO-GADO
(INDONESIAN MIXED VEGETABLE SALAD)

| 1.30 | £ | 275 cals |

Serves 4

vegetable oil, for deep-frying

100 g (4 oz) shelled unsalted
    peanuts

1 small onion, skinned and very
    finely chopped

2 garlic cloves, skinned and
    crushed

2.5–5 ml ($\frac{1}{2}$–1 tsp) chilli powder

5 ml (1 tsp) soft brown sugar

juice of 1 lemon

25 g (1 oz) creamed coconut,
    roughly chopped (optional)

8 small waxy new potatoes

4 small young carrots

100 g (4 oz) cauliflower florets

100 g (4 oz) green cabbage or
    spring greens

100 g (4 oz) French beans

100 g (4 oz) beansprouts

lettuce leaves and slices of
    cucumber and hard-boiled egg,
    to garnish

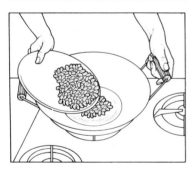

1 Make the peanut sauce. Heat
the oil to 190°C (375°F) in a
wok or deep-fat frier. Lower the
peanuts into the hot oil and deep-
fry for about 5 minutes until the
skins are well browned. Remove
with a slotted spoon and drain on
absorbent kitchen paper.

2 If using a wok, pour off all but
about 30 ml (2 tbsp) of the oil.
(If a deep-fat frier was used to fry
the peanuts, pour 30 ml (2 tbsp) of
the oil into a heavy-based saucepan.) Reheat the oil, add the onion
and garlic and fry gently for about
5 minutes until they are soft and
lightly coloured.

3 Add the chilli powder and stir
fry for 1–2 minutes, then add
350 ml (12 fl oz) water, the sugar,
lemon juice and creamed coconut,
if using. Bring to the boil, stirring
to combine the ingredients
together.

4 Grind the deep-fried peanuts
in a food processor or nut mill,
or with a pestle and mortar. Add
to the sauce and simmer, stirring,
until thickened. Remove and set
aside until ready to serve.

5 Prepare the vegetables for the
salad. Scrub the potatoes and
carrots. Slice the carrots thinly.
Divide the cauliflower into small
sprigs. Cut off any thick, hard
stalks from the cabbage and
discard. Shred the cabbage leaves.
Top and tail the French beans.

6 Boil the potatoes in salted
water for about 20 minutes
until tender. Remove with a
slotted spoon and leave until cool
enough to handle. Add the carrots
to the water and parboil for 4
minutes. Remove the carrots with
a slotted spoon.

7 Blanch the cauliflower and
beans in the water for 3
minutes and remove with a slotted
spoon. Blanch the cabbage and
beansprouts for 1 minute only,
then drain and discard the water.

8 Remove the skin from the
potatoes, then slice the
potatoes into thin rings.

9 Line a large shallow serving
dish or platter with lettuce
leaves. Arrange the prepared
vegetables on top, then garnish
with the slices of cucumber and
hard-boiled egg.

10 Reheat the sauce, stirring
constantly, then pour a
little of the sauce over the salad.
Serve immediately, with the
remaining sauce handed separately
in a jug or bowl.

Menu Suggestion
Serve Gado-Gado on its own as a
lunch dish, with crisply fried
onion rings and prawn crackers.
For 6 people, it would make an
interesting dinner party starter, if
you are serving an Indonesian or
other oriental main course.

GADO-GADO
Literally translated, gado-gado
means 'a mixture'. Ingredients
vary according to availability,
since freshness is the keynote to
all Indonesian salads—if a
particular vegetable is not at its
best, it will not be included.
Some versions of gado-gado have
a fish-flavoured sauce, made by
adding a little shrimp paste or
terasi (available in jars at
oriental stores) to the onion
and garlic in step 2.

CHILLI, AUBERGINE AND RED PEPPER SALAD

| 1.15* | £ | ✳ | 256 cals |

* 30 minutes cooling and 1 hour chilling

Serves 4

2 red peppers

3 medium aubergines, total weight about 700 g (1½ lb)

salt and freshly ground pepper

90 ml (6 tbsp) olive or vegetable oil

2 medium onions, skinned and roughly chopped

15 ml (1 tbsp) chilli seasoning

1.25 ml (¼ tsp) chilli powder

150 ml (¼ pint) dry white wine

30 ml (2 tbsp) tomato purée

15 ml (1 tbsp) lemon juice

15 ml (1 tbsp) wine vinegar

2.5 ml (½ tsp) granulated sugar

chopped fresh parsley, to garnish

1 Put the red peppers whole under a preheated moderate grill and turn them constantly until their skins are charred all over. Put the peppers in a bowl.

2 Trim the aubergines and cut into 2.5 cm (1 inch) cubes. Place in a colander, sprinkling each layer with salt. Cover with a plate, put heavy weights on top and leave to dégorge for about 30 minutes.

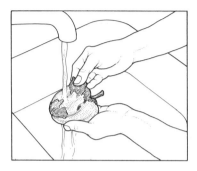

3 Meanwhile, hold the peppers under cold running water and rub the skins off with your fingers. Discard the skins, stems, cores and seeds. Cut the pepper flesh into long, thin shreds and add to the bowl.

4 Rinse the aubergines under cold running water, then pat dry with absorbent kitchen paper. Heat the oil in a heavy-based saucepan. Add the aubergines and onions and fry over moderate heat for 3–4 minutes. Stir in the chilli seasoning and powder. Fry for 1–2 minutes, then add the wine, tomato purée, lemon juice, vinegar, sugar and salt and pepper to taste.

5 Bring to the boil, cover and simmer for 10–12 minutes, or until the aubergine is cooked. Leave to cool for 30 minutes, then turn into a serving bowl.

6 Stir in the red pepper shreds. Cover and chill in the refrigerator for 1 hour. Sprinkle with plenty of chopped parsley before serving.

Menu Suggestion

Serve this smoky flavoured salad with plain roast, barbecued or grilled meat. Or serve for a tasty lunch dish, with hot pitta bread.

GERMAN POTATO SALAD

| 0.40 | £ | 402 cals |

Serves 4

900 g (2 lb) waxy potatoes

salt and freshly ground pepper

4 streaky bacon rashers, rinded and chopped

1 large Spanish onion, skinned and finely chopped

2 celery sticks, trimmed and finely chopped

1 green eating apple, peeled, cored and chopped

100 ml (4 fl oz) dry white wine

30 ml (2 tbsp) white wine vinegar

2.5 ml ($\frac{1}{2}$ tsp) sugar

1.25 ml ($\frac{1}{4}$ tsp) paprika

30 ml (2 tbsp) olive oil

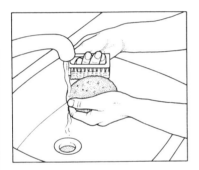

1 Scrub the potatoes, but do not peel them. Place in a pan, cover with cold water and add 5 ml (1 tsp) salt. Bring to the boil, then cover the pan and simmer for 20 minutes or until tender.

2 Meanwhile, fry the bacon in its own fat in a non-stick saucepan until crisp. Remove it with a slotted spoon and set aside on a plate.

3 Add the onion and celery to the bacon fat in the pan. Fry gently for about 10 minutes until soft and lightly coloured, then add the remaining ingredients, with salt and pepper to taste. Bring to the boil, stirring, then remove from the heat.

4 Drain the potatoes and leave until cold enough to handle. Peel off the skins, then place the potatoes in a bowl.

5 Pour over the hot dressing, add the bacon and sprinkle over the oil. Toss the potatoes gently until thoroughly coated, then leave to cool. Taste and adjust seasoning before serving.

Menu Suggestion
German Potato Salad is good with frankfurters or a frying sausage such as bratwürst. Serve for a German-style lunch, with tankards of lager or beer, and hunks of rye bread.

GERMAN POTATO SALAD
Waxy potatoes are best for salads because they keep their shape and do not disintegrate during cooking. There are three varieties of 'second-early' potatoes which are waxy and therefore excellent in salads: Estima have a light yellow skin and flesh, Maris Peer are white, and Wilja are pale yellow at the beginning of the season but darker as they mature. Maincrop potatoes do not make the best salads because they have lost some of their water.

For maximum nutritive value, cook potatoes in their skins. They are a valuable source of vitamins, including vitamin C and vitamin B6, carbohydrate, dietary fibre and copper, with some protein, calcium and iron.

BEETROOT SALAD WITH MINT

0.15*	£	43–64 cals

* plus 2–3 hours or overnight chilling

Serves 4–6

120 ml (8 tbsp) chopped fresh mint

700 g (1½ lb) cooked beetroot

150 ml (¼ pint) malt vinegar

5 ml (1 tsp) granulated sugar

salt and freshly ground pepper

2 medium onions, skinned and finely sliced into rings

1 Put 90 ml (6 tbsp) of the mint in a bowl and pour over 150 ml (¼ pint) boiling water. Leave to stand for 2–3 minutes.

2 Peel the beetroot and slice thinly. Place in a large shallow dish. Add the vinegar and sugar to the mint and water with salt and pepper to taste. Pour over the beetroot. Cover and chill in the refrigerator for at least 2–3 hours or overnight.

3 To serve, place alternate layers of beetroot and onion in a serving dish. Pour over the mint dressing and garnish with the remaining chopped fresh mint. Serve chilled.

Menu Suggestion

Beetroot salads go especially well with roast lamb, turkey and duck, and cold meats such as ham and salami.

BEETROOT SALAD WITH MINT

Did you know that the Victorians were extremely fond of beetroots? They not only used them as a salad vegetable, but also dried and ground them with coffee to make the coffee go further, pickled them, made them into wine, candied them as sweets—and made them into a lotion for rinsing hair!

RICE SALAD

| 0.40* | £ | 577 cals |

* plus 1 hour cooling

Serves 4

| 275 g (10 oz) long grain brown rice |
| salt and freshly ground pepper |
| 1 head of fennel |
| 1 red pepper |
| 175 g (6 oz) beansprouts |
| 75 g (3 oz) cashew nuts |
| 90 ml (6 tbsp) corn or vegetable oil |
| finely grated rind and juice of 1 large orange |
| few orange segments, to garnish |

1 Cook the brown rice in plenty of boiling salted water for 30 minutes (or according to packet instructions), until tender but firm to the bite.

2 Meanwhile, prepare the remaining ingredients. Trim the fennel, reserving a few feathery tops for the garnish. Cut the top off the red pepper and remove the core and seeds. Wash the pepper and pat dry with absorbent kitchen paper.

3 Chop the fennel and red pepper finely. Wash the beansprouts and drain well. Chop the cashew nuts roughly.

4 In a jug, whisk the oil, orange rind and juice together, with salt and pepper to taste.

5 Drain the rice thoroughly, then turn into a bowl. Add the dressing while the rice is still hot and toss well to combine. Leave to stand for about 1 hour, or until the rice is cold.

6 Add the prepared vegetables and nuts to the rice and toss well to mix. Taste and adjust seasoning. Turn the salad into a serving bowl and garnish with the reserved fennel tops and the orange segments. Serve at room temperature.

Menu Suggestion
This nutty brown rice salad has a tangy orange dressing, which makes it the perfect accompaniment to rich meat dishes such as pork and duck. Alternatively, it can be served with other vegetable salads for a vegetarian meal—it goes particularly well with green salad ingredients such as chicory, endive, lettuce and watercress.

GRAPE, WATERCRESS AND STILTON SALAD

0.20*	£ £	379 cals

* plus 1 hour chilling

Serves 4

| 175 g (6 oz) black grapes |
| 1 bunch watercress |
| 45 ml (3 tbsp) vegetable oil |
| 15 ml (1 tbsp) lemon juice |
| 5 ml (1 tsp) poppy seeds |
| pinch of caster sugar |
| salt and freshly ground pepper |
| 225 g (8 oz) Stilton cheese |

5 To serve, toss together the grapes, watercress, Stilton and dressing. Serve immediately.

Menu Suggestion
This special salad is excellent for buffet parties served with a selection of other salads, quiches, pâtés and cold meats.

1 Halve the grapes and remove the pips. Place in a bowl, cover and chill in the refrigerator.

2 Trim the watercress of any tough root ends. Wash thoroughly, drain and pat dry.

3 In a jug, whisk together the oil, lemon juice, poppy seeds, sugar and salt and pepper to taste.

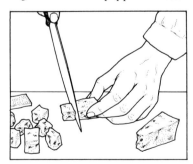

4 Cut the rind off the Stilton and cut the cheese into 1.5 cm ($\frac{3}{4}$ inch) cubes. Toss well in the prepared dressing to coat completely. Cover and chill in the refrigerator for 1 hour.

GREEK SALAD

0.20*	£	214 cals

* plus 2–3 hours or overnight chilling

Serves 4

| $\frac{1}{2}$ large cucumber |
| salt and freshly ground pepper |
| 450 g (1 lb) firm ripe tomatoes |
| 1 medium red onion |
| 18 black olives |
| 125 g (4 oz) Feta cheese, cut into cubes |
| 60 ml (4 tbsp) olive oil |
| 15 ml (1 tbsp) lemon juice |
| good pinch of dried oregano |

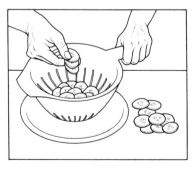

1 Peel the cucumber and slice thinly. Put into a colander or sieve, sprinkle with a little salt and leave to stand for about 15 minutes.

2 Slice the tomatoes thinly. Skin the onion and slice into thin rings. Rinse the cucumber under cold running water, drain and pat dry with absorbent kitchen paper.

3 Arrange the cucumber, tomatoes and onion in a serving dish. Scatter the olives and cubed cheese over the top.

4 In a bowl, whisk together the oil, lemon juice, oregano and salt and pepper to taste. Spoon the dressing over the salad, cover tightly with cling film and chill for 2–3 hours, or overnight. Allow to come to room temperature for 30 minutes before serving.

Menu Suggestion
In Greece, this kind of salad is usually served as a first course with hot pitta bread, or as a side dish to barbecued kebabs.

STUFFED VEGETABLE PLATTER

`2.20*` ⏲ ⏲ £ £ `852 cals`

* plus cooling and overnight chilling

Serves 4

| 200 ml (7 fl oz) olive oil |
| 1 large Spanish onion, skinned and very finely chopped |
| 2 garlic cloves, skinned and crushed |
| 1 bunch of fresh parsley |
| 225 g (8 oz) Italian risotto rice, cooked |
| 20 ml (4 tsp) tomato purée |
| 50 g (2 oz) pine nuts |
| 75 g (3 oz) raisins |
| 2.5 ml ($\frac{1}{2}$ tsp) ground allspice |
| salt and freshly ground pepper |
| 4 medium courgettes |
| 4 small squat peppers (preferably different colours) |
| 4 small very firm continental or beefsteak tomatoes |

1 First prepare the stuffing. Heat 60 ml (4 tbsp) of the oil in a heavy-based saucepan, add the onion and garlic and fry gently for about 10 minutes until very soft.

2 Trim the parsley stalks, then chop the parsley very finely. Add the rice to the onion with the tomato purée, chopped parsley, nuts, raisins, allspice and salt and pepper to taste. Stir well to mix all the ingredients together, then remove the pan from the heat and set aside.

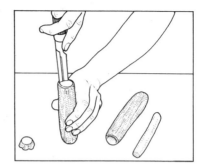

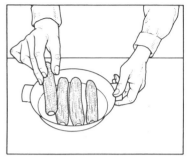

3 Using an apple corer, scoop out the flesh from the courgettes. Work from the stalk end, taking care not to break the skin of the courgettes and to leave the opposite ends intact. Mix the courgette flesh into the stuffing. Sprinkle salt inside the courgettes and leave to drain while preparing the other vegetables.

4 Cut a slice off the top of each pepper and reserve. Remove the cores and seeds and discard, then wash the peppers and pat dry with absorbent kitchen paper.

5 Cut the tops off the tomatoes and reserve. With a sharp-edged teaspoon, scoop out the flesh. Mix the flesh with the stuffing. Sprinkle the insides of the tomatoes with salt and stand upside down to drain.

6 Stuff the vegetables with the filling. Wrap the open ends of the courgettes with foil. Replace the tops on the peppers and tomatoes.

7 Brush the inside of a flame-proof gratin dish liberally with some of the remaining olive oil. Arrange the courgettes side by side in the dish. Brush 2 heavy-based saucepans liberally with oil; stand the peppers and tomatoes in them, keeping them separate.

8 Sprinkle with the remaining oil and salt and pepper to taste, then pour in enough cold water to come halfway up the vegetables. Bring slowly to the boil, then cover and simmer very gently. Allow 30 minutes for the tomatoes, 45 minutes for the courgettes and peppers. Leave to cool in the pans, then chill in the refrigerator overnight.

9 To serve, lift the vegetables carefully out of the cooking liquid and arrange attractively on a large serving platter. Moisten with a little of the cooking liquid, if liked. Serve chilled.

Menu Suggestion
Stuffed mixed vegetables are a favourite starter in the Middle East, but this quantity is ample to serve 4 people for a main course, and would make an impressive cold lunch dish in summer, when courgettes, peppers and tomatoes are at their best. Serve with French bread or warm pitta bread, to mop up the juices.

VEGETABLE TERRINE

| 2.30 | 🍴 🍴 £ | 250–334 cals |

Serves 6–8

900 g (2 lb) turnips, peeled and cut into chunks

450 g (1 lb) carrots, peeled and sliced

450 g (1 lb) fresh spinach, trimmed, or 300 g (10.6 oz) packet frozen spinach

50 g (2 oz) butter or margarine

1 medium onion, skinned and thinly sliced

350 g (12 oz) flat mushrooms, sliced

finely grated rind and juice of ½ lemon

4 eggs

salt and freshly ground white pepper

1.25 ml (¼ tsp) ground coriander

1.25 ml (¼ tsp) freshly grated nutmeg

30 ml (2 tbsp) chopped fresh parsley

2 ripe tomatoes, skinned

300 ml (½ pint) Vinaigrette (page 151)

1 Put the turnips into a medium saucepan, cover with cold water and bring to the boil. Lower the heat and simmer for 10–15 minutes, until completely tender.

2 Meanwhile, put the carrots in a separate saucepan and cover with cold water. Bring to the boil and cook for 10 minutes or until completely tender. Drain both turnips and carrots.

3 Wash the fresh spinach in several changes of cold water. Place in a saucepan with only the water that clings to the leaves. Cook gently for 5 minutes until wilted, 7–10 minutes if using frozen spinach. Drain well.

4 Melt 40 g (1½ oz) of the butter in a frying pan, add the onion and fry gently for about 10 minutes until very soft. Add the mushrooms and fry, stirring constantly, for a further 5 minutes. Stir in the lemon rind and juice.

5 Put the mushroom mixture in a blender or food processor and work until smooth. Transfer to a small heavy-based pan. Cook over moderate heat, stirring constantly, until all the liquid has evaporated and the purée is fairly thick and dry. Watch that the mixture does not catch and burn.

6 Purée and dry the turnips, carrots and spinach in the same way and place each purée in a separate bowl. Add 1 egg to each purée and mix well. Season each with salt and pepper to taste. Stir the coriander into the carrot purée, the grated nutmeg into the spinach and the chopped parsley into the mushroom.

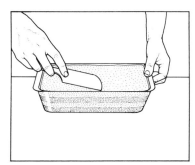

7 Brush a 1.1 litre (2 pint) terrine or loaf tin with the remaining butter. Put a layer of turnip purée in the bottom, making sure it is quite level. Cover with a layer of carrot, followed by spinach and finally mushroom. Cover the tin tightly with foil.

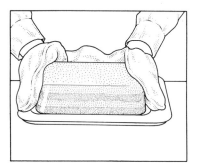

8 Place the terrine in a roasting tin and pour in enough hot water to come three-quarters of the way up the sides of the terrine. Bake in the oven at 180°C (350°F) mark 4 for 1 hour 20 minutes or until firm. Remove and allow to cool slightly, then turn out carefully on to a serving plate.

9 Just before serving, put the tomatoes and vinaigrette in a blender or food processor and work until smooth. Do not let the dressing stand before serving or it will separate.

10 Serve the terrine hot or cold, cut into slices, on top of the tomato vinaigrette.

Note Other vegetables may be used when in season, such as cauliflower, fennel, watercress, parsnips and even peas. Try to balance colour and flavour.

Menu Suggestion
Vegetable Terrine can be served as a dinner party starter or for a light lunch dish. In either case, it is delicious served with a crusty French stick or granary bread.

Hot Accompani- ments

Vegetable accompaniments so often get forgotten, and yet they are a vital part of any main course. This chapter will fire your imagination, and turn your vegetable accompaniments into dishes to be savoured in their own right.

TRIO OF VEGETABLE PURÉES

| 0.40 | 249 cals |

Serves 4

450 g (1 lb) carrots, scrubbed or
   peeled and roughly chopped

450 g (1 lb) parsnips or turnips,
   peeled and roughly chopped

salt and freshly ground pepper

350 g (12 oz) frozen peas

few fresh mint sprigs

5 ml (1 tsp) lemon juice

pinch of granulated sugar

40 g ($1\frac{1}{2}$ oz) butter or margarine

45 ml (3 tbsp) single or double
   cream

1.25 ml ($\frac{1}{4}$ tsp) ground coriander

good pinch of freshly grated
   nutmeg

1 Cook the carrots and parsnips or turnips in separate pans of boiling salted water for about 20 minutes or until tender. At the same time, cook the frozen peas in boiling salted water according to packet instructions, with the mint sprigs, lemon juice and sugar.

2 Drain the vegetables, keeping them separate. Put the peas and mint in a blender or food processor with one-third of the butter and 15 ml (1 tbsp) of the cream. Work to a smooth purée, then add salt and pepper to taste.

3 Rinse out the machine, then add the carrots, another third of the butter, 15 ml (1 tbsp) cream and the coriander. Work to a smooth purée, then add salt and pepper to taste.

4 Repeat puréeing with the parsnips or turnips, the remaining butter and cream and the nutmeg. Add salt and pepper to taste.

5 Return all 3 purées to individual pans and reheat gently, stirring all the time. Spoon into 3 warmed serving bowls or in 3 or more sections in 1 large bowl. Serve immediately.

Menu Suggestion
Vegetable purées make an attractive alternative to plain boiled or mashed vegetables, especially for Sunday lunch or when entertaining.

TRIO OF VEGETABLE PURÉE

Garnish the top of the carrot purée with sprigs of fresh coriander, the pea purée with mint and the parsnips or turnips with a sprinkling of freshly grated nutmeg.

   Ground coriander goes especially well with carrots, as do most Indian spices. For a spicier flavour, buy whole coriander seeds fresh from an Indian grocer and dry roast them for a few minutes in a non-stick, or heavy cast iron, frying pan. When the seeds begin to pop and burst, turn them into a mortar and grind to a fine powder with a pestle. Use fresh for maximum flavour, or store in an airtight container and use within a few weeks. If you are fond of coriander, splinkle the carrot purée liberally with the freshly chopped herb before serving.

SWISS CHALET POTATOES WITH CREAM AND CHEESE

| 1.20 | £ £ | 529–793 cals |

Serves 4–6

1.4 kg (3 lb) even-sized small
   potatoes, peeled

salt and freshly ground pepper

300 ml ($\frac{1}{2}$ pint) double cream

1–2 garlic cloves, skinned and
   crushed

good pinch of freshly grated
   nutmeg

75 g (3 oz) Gruyère or Emmental
   cheese, grated

75 g (3 oz) Parmesan cheese,
   freshly grated

1 Parboil the potatoes in a large saucepan of salted water for 10 minutes. Drain well.

2 Stand the potatoes upright in a buttered baking dish. Mix the cream with the garlic, nutmeg and salt and pepper to taste, then pour over the potatoes.

3 Mix the 2 cheeses together and sprinkle over the potatoes to cover them completely. Bake, uncovered, in the oven at 190°C (375°F) mark 5 for 1 hour, or until the potatoes feel tender when pierced with a skewer. Serve hot, straight from the dish.

Menu Suggestion
This luscious potato dish is very rich, and therefore best reserved for special occasions. It would go particularly well with a plain roast joint and Trio of Vegetable Purées (page 93).

SWISS CHALET POTATOES WITH CREAM AND CHEESE

The Swiss cheeses Gruyère and Emmental are expensive, but their uniquely sweet and nutty flavour makes them well worth the extra cost for a potato dish such as this one—and you only need a small amount to appreciate their special flavour.

Genuine Gruyère cheese has the alpenhorn symbol and the red 'Switzerland' stamp on its rind; it is full in flavour, which comes from its long ripening period of up to 12 months. It is a moist cheese, with few holes when cut, and is excellent for melting, which is why it is the traditional cheese to use in fondue.

Emmental is a relation of Gruyère and also carries the red Switzerland stamp on its rind. It differs from Gruyère in that it is milder in flavour, with holes the size of cherries. Both Gruyère and Emmental are widely available.

GREEK-STYLE NEW POTATOES

| 0.45 | 🗋 | £ | 280 cals |

Serves 4

1 kg (2 lb) small new potatoes,
    preferably Cyprus

250 ml (8 fl oz) vegetable oil

125 ml (4 fl oz) white or red wine
    (see box)

60 ml (4 tbsp) chopped fresh
    coriander, mint or parsley

salt and freshly ground pepper

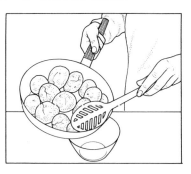

1 Scrub the potatoes clean, leaving them whole. Pat the potatoes thoroughly dry with a clean tea towel.

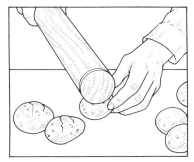

2 With a meat mallet, hit each potato once or twice so that the flesh breaks slightly. Heat the oil in a heavy-based deep frying pan, skillet or saucepan until a stale bread cube turns golden in 2–3 seconds.

3 Add the potatoes to the hot oil and fry over moderate heat, turning them frequently, until golden brown on all sides.

4 Pour off the oil, then pour the wine over the potatoes. Add half of the chopped coriander and a liberal sprinkling of salt and pepper. Shake the pan to combine the ingredients, then cover and simmer for about 15 minutes, until the potatoes are tender.

5 Turn the potatoes into a warmed serving dish and sprinkle with the remaining coriander. Serve immediately.

Menu Suggestion
These tasty potatoes are good with plain roast or grilled lamb; they are also excellent with barbecued meat, especially lamb kebabs.

GREEK-STYLE NEW POTATOES

For an authentic flavour to these potatoes, cook them in Greek retsina wine. Most retsina is white, but you can use either white or red, depending on which is easier to obtain. Retsina, or resinated wine, is something of an acquired taste. It has a strong bouquet and flavour of turpentine, which was discovered almost my mistake.

Originally, some hundreds of years ago, the wine jars or amphorae were sealed with a mixture of resin and plaster, and the flavour of the seal naturally made its way into the wine. The Greeks became so fond of the taste, that they began to add pine resin to the must during fermentation, which resulted in a heady wine with a distinctive flavour.

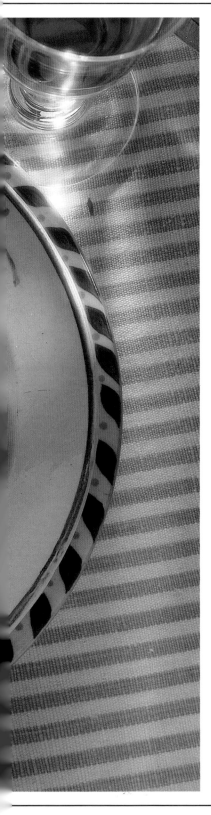

COLCANNON
(IRISH MASHED POTATOES WITH KALE AND LEEKS)

0.35	211 cals

Serves 6

450 g (1 lb) potatoes, peeled and
quartered

salt and freshly ground pepper

450 g (1 lb) kale or cabbage, cored
and shredded

2 small leeks, sliced and washed

150 ml (¼ pint) milk or double
cream

50 g (2 oz) butter or margarine

melted butter, to serve

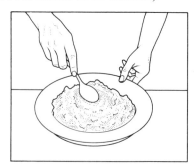

1 Cook the potatoes in boiling
salted water for 15–20 minutes
until tender. Meanwhile, cook the
kale in a separate saucepan of
boiling salted water for 5–10
minutes until tender. Drain both
potatoes and kale.

2 Put the leeks and milk or
cream in a saucepan and
simmer gently for 10–15 minutes
until soft.

3 Put the leeks in a large bowl,
add the potatoes, then the kale,
butter and salt and pepper to taste.
Beat together over gentle heat
until the mixture is thoroughly
blended.

4 Mound the mixture on a
warmed serving dish and make
a hollow in the top. Pour a little
melted butter into the hollow, to
be mixed in at the last minute.

Menu Suggestion
Serve Colcannon for a mid-week
family meal with chops or
sausages.

COLCANNON

In Ireland, Colcannon is
traditionally eaten on All
Hallows' Day, which is
Hallowe'en, 31 October. Older
recipes were made with kale,
which was cooked with bacon to
make it really tasty, but
nowadays cabbage is often used
or a mixture of kale and
cabbage. Minced onion can be
substituted for the leeks, if
leeks are not available. Although
Colcannon is essentially a
homely dish, the addition of
cream and butter makes it quite
rich and special. There is a
superstition surrounding
Colcannon in Ireland, much the
same as the one associated with
plum pudding in Britain. Years
ago, Irish cooks are said to have
hidden gold wedding rings in the
mixture, and it was believed
that the finder would be married
within the year. If the cook hid a
thimble, however, this would
mean the finder would remain
unmarried.

RÖSTI
(SWISS POTATO CAKE)

0.45*	🍴	292–585 cals

* plus 10 minutes cooling

Serves 2–4

700 g (1½ lb) old potatoes, scrubbed

salt and freshly ground pepper

75 g (3 oz) butter, margarine or lard

1 small onion, skinned and finely chopped

1 Quarter any large potatoes and put in a saucepan of salted water. Bring to the boil and cook for 7 minutes. Drain well, leave to cool for about 10 minutes until cool enough to handle, then remove the skins.

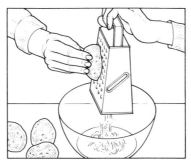

2 Using a hand grater, grate the potatoes into a bowl. Melt 25 g (1 oz) of the butter in a frying pan, add the onion and fry gently for about 5 minutes until soft but not coloured.

3 Add the remaining butter to the onion and heat until melted. Add the grated potato and sprinkle with salt and pepper. Fry the potatoes, turning them constantly until they have absorbed all the fat.

4 Using a palette knife, form the potato into a neat, flat cake and flatten the top. Sprinkle with 15 ml (1 tbsp) water, cover the pan and cook gently for 15–20 minutes, until the underside is golden brown. Shake the pan occasionally to prevent the potato sticking to the bottom of the pan.

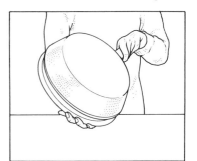

5 When cooked, place a large warmed serving plate on top of the frying pan. Invert the pan and turn the potatoes on to the plate so that the golden side is uppermost. Serve immediately, cut into wedges. Alternatively, serve straight from the pan, cut into wedges and inverted.

Menu Suggestion
Rösti is one of the most delicious of potato dishes. Serve for a special occasion, with grilled or barbecued steak.

RED CABBAGE AND APPLE CASSEROLE

| 3.30 | £ | 121–182 cals |

Serves 4–6

700 g (1½ lb) red cabbage

2 cooking apples

1 large Spanish onion

15 g (½ oz) butter or margarine

50 g (2 oz) raisins

salt and freshly ground pepper

30 ml (2 tbsp) granulated sugar

60 ml (4 tbsp) white wine or wine vinegar

30 ml (2 tbsp) port (optional)

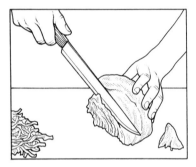

1 Shred the cabbage finely, discarding the thick central stalk. Peel and core the apples and slice them thinly. Skin the onion and slice thinly.

2 Brush the inside of a large ovenproof dish with the butter. Put a layer of shredded cabbage in the bottom and cover with a layer of sliced apple and onion. Sprinkle over a few of the raisins and season with salt and pepper to taste.

3 In a jug, mix the sugar with the wine, and the port if using. Sprinkle a little of this mixture over the ingredients in the dish.

4 Continue layering the ingredients in the dish until they are all used up. Cover the dish and bake in the oven at 150°C (300°F) mark 2 for 3 hours. Taste and adjust seasoning, then turn into a warmed serving dish. Serve the casserole hot.

Menu Suggestion
This vegetable casserole has a tangy fruit flavour, which makes it the ideal accompaniment for rich meats. It is especially good with roast pork, duck, pheasant and partridge, and would also go well with the festive turkey at Christmastime.

RED CABBAGE AND APPLE CASSEROLE
Casseroles of cabbage like this one are popular in northern France, particularly in Ardennes, which borders on Belgium. Both white and red cabbage are used, but with white cabbage dry white wine is usually preferred to the red used here. A spoonful or two of redcurrant jelly is sometimes added to red cabbage casseroles. Substitute this for the port if liked, plus a few crushed juniper berries, which are a favourite flavouring ingredient in northern Europe.

This quantity of cabbage makes enough for 4–6 good helpings; reheat any leftover casserole for another supper as it will have an excellent flavour. If there is any left over, refrigerate it in a covered bowl overnight, then the next day, toss it in a pan with a little butter until hot.

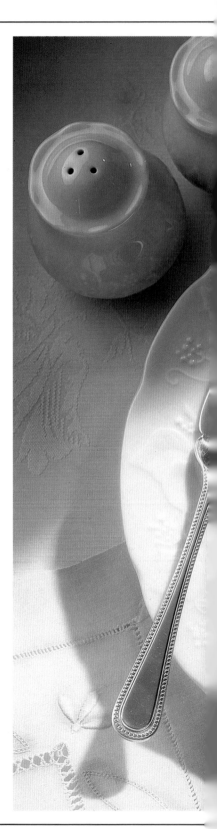

Tian à la Provençale
(Aubergine Gratin)

| 1.15 | 🍲 £ ✳* | 428 cals |

* freeze before baking at step 6

Serves 4

450 g (1 lb) aubergines

salt and freshly ground pepper

25 g (1 oz) butter or margarine

25 g (1 oz) plain flour

300 ml ($\frac{1}{2}$ pint) milk

60 ml (4 tbsp) Parmesan cheese, freshly grated

1.25 ml ($\frac{1}{4}$ tsp) freshly grated nutmeg

about 150 ml ($\frac{1}{4}$ pint) olive or vegetable oil

350 g (12 oz) tomatoes, skinned and sliced

2 garlic cloves, skinned and roughly chopped

2 eggs, beaten

1 Slice the aubergines thinly, then place in a colander, sprinkling each layer with salt. Cover with a plate, place heavy weights on top and leave to dégorge for 30 minutes.

2 Meanwhile, melt the butter in a saucepan, add the flour and cook gently, stirring, for 1–2 minutes. Remove from the heat and gradually blend in the milk. Bring to the boil, stirring constantly, then simmer for 3 minutes until thick and smooth. Add half of the cheese, the nutmeg and salt and pepper to taste, stir well to mix, then remove from the heat.

3 Rinse the aubergine slices under cold running water, then pat dry with absorbent kitchen paper.

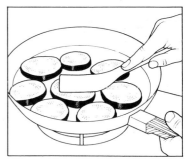

4 Pour enough oil into a heavy-based frying pan to cover the base. Heat until very hot, then add a layer of aubergine slices. Fry over moderate heat until golden brown on both sides, turning once. Remove with a slotted spoon and drain on absorbent kitchen paper. Repeat with more oil and aubergines.

5 Arrange alternate layers of aubergines and tomatoes in an oiled gratin or baking dish. Sprinkle each layer with garlic, a little salt and plenty of pepper.

6 Beat the eggs into the sauce, then pour slowly into the dish. Sprinkle the remaining cheese evenly over the top. Bake in the oven at 200°C (400°F) mark 6 for 20 minutes or until golden brown and bubbling. Serve hot.

Menu Suggestion
This substantial, creamy vegetable dish is excellent served with roast lamb or grilled chops. It also makes a tasty vegetarian dinner with potatoes and a salad.

HERBY COURGETTE FINGERS WITH CREAM

0.30*	£	147–196 cals

* plus 1 hour to dégorge

Serves 6–8

900 g (2 lb) small or medium courgettes

salt and freshly ground pepper

50 g (2 oz) butter

1–2 garlic cloves, skinned and crushed

150 ml ($\frac{1}{4}$ pint) vegetable stock or water

20 ml (4 tsp) chopped fresh basil or 10 ml (2 tsp) dried

150 ml ($\frac{1}{4}$ pint) double cream

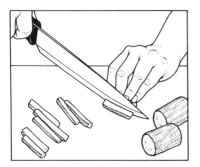

1 Trim the courgettes, then cut them into neat strips about 5 cm (2 inches) long and 0.5 cm ($\frac{1}{4}$ inch) wide.

2 Put the courgette strips in a colander, sprinkling each layer with salt. Cover with a plate, place heavy weights on top and leave to dégorge for 1 hour.

3 Rinse the courgette strips thoroughly under cold running water, then pat dry in a clean tea towel.

4 Melt half of the butter in a heavy-based saucepan, add the courgettes and garlic and toss over moderate heat for a few minutes.

5 Pour in the stock, then add half of the basil with salt and pepper to taste. Cover the pan and simmer gently for 5 minutes or until the courgettes are tender but still with some crunch. Transfer the courgettes to a warmed serving dish with a slotted spoon, cover and keep hot.

6 Increase the heat and boil the liquid to reduce slightly. Add the cream and the remaining butter and basil. Simmer until the sauce is of a coating consistency. Taste and adjust seasoning, then pour over the courgettes. Serve immediately.

Menu Suggestion

Serve this creamy vegetable dish in summer when courgettes are plentiful; it goes especially well with lamb and chicken dishes.

HERBY COURGETTE FINGERS WITH CREAM

Courgettes are members of the same cucurbit family as pumpkins, gourds, marrows, squashes and cucumbers. They are believed to have been eaten originally by the American Indians, who ground down the seeds of gourds rather than eating the flesh. Marrows were known in Roman times, and courgettes were cultivated from them.

It is a good idea to dégorge courgettes before cooking, as in this recipe. They are a watery vegetable, and can dilute sauces such as this creamy one if they are not dégorged beforehand. Older courgettes can also be bitter, another reason for extracting the juice before cooking. Always rinse them thoroughly after dégorging, or the finished dish may be salty.

TOFU AND VEGETABLES IN SPICY COCONUT SAUCE

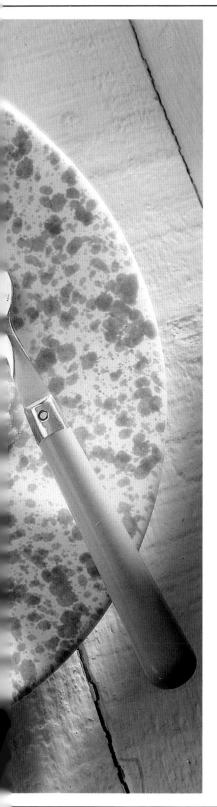

| 1.00 | 🍲 | £ | 271 cals |

Serves 4

75 g (3 oz) creamed coconut

225 g (8 oz) firm or pressed tofu (beancurd)

vegetable oil, for deep frying, plus 45 ml (3 tbsp)

6 spring onions, trimmed and finely chopped

2.5 cm (1 inch) piece of fresh root ginger, peeled and finely chopped

1 garlic clove, skinned and crushed

2.5 ml ($\frac{1}{2}$ tsp) turmeric

2.5 ml ($\frac{1}{2}$ tsp) chilli powder

30 ml (2 tbsp) soy sauce

4 medium carrots, peeled and cut into matchstick strips

225 g (8 oz) cauliflower florets, separated into small sprigs

175 g (6 oz) French beans, topped and tailed

175 g (6 oz) beansprouts

salt and freshly ground pepper

1 First make the coconut milk. Cut the creamed coconut into small pieces and place in a measuring jug. Pour in boiling water up to the 900 ml (1$\frac{1}{2}$ pint) mark. Stir until dissolved, then strain through a muslin-lined sieve. Set aside.

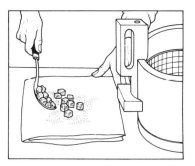

2 Drain the tofu and cut into cubes. Pat thoroughly dry with absorbent kitchen paper. Heat the oil to 190°C (375°F) in a wok or deep-fat frier. Deep-fry the cubes of tofu in the hot oil until golden brown on all sides, turning them frequently with a slotted spoon. Remove and drain on absorbent kitchen paper.

3 Heat the 45 ml (3 tbsp) oil in a heavy-based saucepan or flameproof casserole. Add the spring onions, ginger and garlic and fry gently for about 5 minutes until softened.

4 Add the turmeric and chilli powder and stir fry for 1–2 minutes, then add the coconut milk and soy sauce and bring to the boil, stirring all the time. Add carrots and cauliflower. Simmer, uncovered, for 10 minutes.

5 Add the French beans and simmer for a further 5 minutes, then add the tofu and beansprouts and heat through. Add salt and pepper to taste, then turn into a warmed serving dish. Serve immediately.

Menu Suggestion

This Indonesian-style vegetable dish makes the perfect accompaniment to any oriental meat or poultry dish. It is also excellent — and extremely nutritious — served with rice or Chinese egg noodles for a vegetarian meal.

CHINESE VEGETABLE STIR-FRY

0.30	£	267 cals

Serves 4

350 g (12 oz) mangetout

2 large red peppers

1 bunch of spring onions

225 g (8 oz) can water chestnuts

5 cm (2 inch) piece of fresh root ginger

1–2 garlic cloves

30 ml (2 tbsp) vegetable oil

15 ml (1 tbsp) sesame oil (optional)

30 ml (2 tbsp) dry sherry

30 ml (2 tbsp) soy sauce

10 ml (2 tsp) honey or soft brown sugar

10 ml (2 tsp) tomato purée

salt and freshly ground pepper

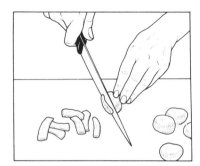

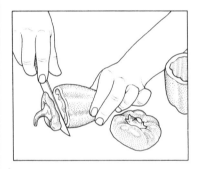

1 First prepare the vegetables. Top and tail the mangetout. Cut the tops off the peppers, remove the cores and seeds and wash thoroughly inside and out.

2 Pat the peppers dry with absorbent kitchen paper, then shred the flesh finely. Trim and shred the spring onions.

3 Drain the water chestnuts, rinse under cold running water, then shred finely.

4 Peel the root ginger, then cut the flesh into matchstick lengths. Skin and crush the garlic.

5 Heat the oils in a wok or deep, heavy-based frying pan. Add the spring onions, ginger and garlic and stir fry for 2–3 minutes. Add the remaining prepared vegetables and stir fry to mix them together.

6 In a bowl or jug, mix together the remaining ingredients, with salt and pepper to taste. Pour over the vegetables, moisten with about 60 ml (4 tbsp) water and mix well. Cook for about 5 minutes, stirring constantly, until the mangetout and red peppers are tender but still crunchy. Transfer to a warmed serving bowl and serve immediately.

Menu Suggestion
Serve this colourful stir-fried dish with pork, beef or duck, or with steamed or fried fish. Chinese egg noodles can be stir fried with the vegetables, or served separately.

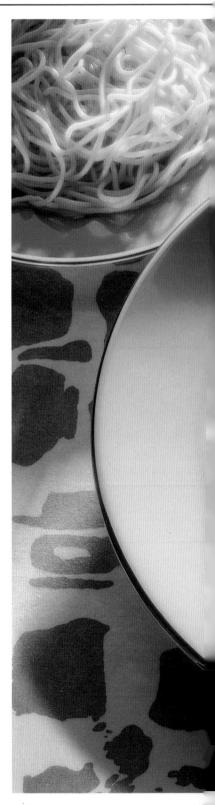

CHINESE VEGETABLE STIR-FRY

Fresh water chestnuts are sometimes available in oriental specialist shops, but canned water chestnuts can be bought from most large supermarkets and delicatessens. Water chestnuts are not actually chestnuts, but the sweet root-bulb of an Asian marsh plant. The canned variety are ready peeled and have a good crunchy texture. They are bland tasting, so need to be combined with strong-tasting foods.

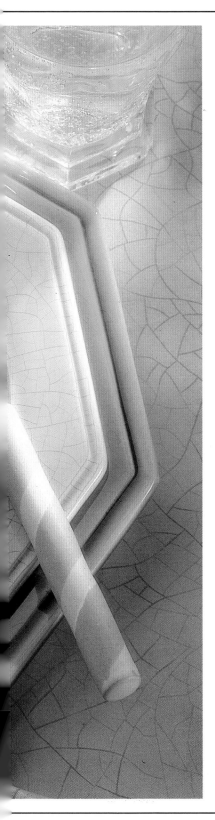

CELERIAC WITH TOMATO SAUCE

| 1.10 | £ ✳* | 295 cals |

* freeze before baking at end of step 6

Serves 4

60 ml (4 tbsp) olive oil

1 large onion, skinned and finely chopped

3 garlic cloves, skinned and crushed

350 g (12 oz) ripe tomatoes, skinned and finely chopped

15 ml (1 tbsp) tomato purée

30 ml (2 tbsp) red wine or red wine vinegar

60 ml (4 tbsp) chopped fresh parsley

5 ml (1 tsp) ground cinnamon

1 bay leaf

salt and freshly ground pepper

2 heads of celeriac, total weight about 900 g (2 lb)

5 ml (1 tsp) lemon juice

50 g (2 oz) dried brown or white breadcrumbs

50 g (2 oz) Parmesan cheese, freshly grated

1 Prepare the tomato sauce. Heat the oil in a heavy-based saucepan, add the onion and garlic and fry gently for about 10 minutes until very soft and lightly coloured.

2 Add the tomatoes, tomato purée, wine, parsley, cinnamon, bay leaf and salt and pepper to taste. Add 450 ml ($\frac{3}{4}$ pint) hot water and bring to the boil, stirring with a wooden spoon to break up the tomatoes.

3 Lower the heat, cover and simmer the tomato sauce for 30 minutes, stirring occasionally.

4 Meanwhile, peel the celeriac, then cut into chunky pieces. As you prepare the celeriac, place the pieces in a bowl of water to which the lemon juice has been added, to prevent discoloration.

5 Drain the celeriac, then plunge quickly into a large pan of boiling salted water. Return to the boil and blanch for 10 minutes.

6 Drain the celeriac well, then put in an ovenproof dish. Pour over the tomato sauce (discarding the bay leaf), then sprinkle the breadcrumbs and cheese evenly over the top.

7 Bake the celeriac in the oven at 190°C (375°F) mark 5 for 30 minutes, until the celeriac is tender when pierced with a skewer and the topping is golden brown. Serve hot, straight from the dish.

Menu Suggestion
With its strongly flavoured tomato sauce, this gratin of celeriac tastes good with plain roast or grilled meat and poultry. It also makes a tasty vegetarian dish in its own right, served with a nutty pilaf such as Burghul Wheat Pilaf (page 124).

Pulses, Grains and Nuts

Include pulses and grains in your recipe repertoire and you will add extra nutritional value—at a fraction of the cost of other high-protein foods. The dishes in this chapter come from all over the world, and will lend your cooking an international air— without breaking the bank.

RED KIDNEY BEAN HOT POT

2.35* | 537 cals

* plus overnight soaking

Serves 2

125 g (4 oz) dried red kidney beans, soaked in cold water overnight

1 medium onion

125 g (4 oz) celery, trimmed

125 g (4 oz) carrots, peeled

125 g (4 oz) courgettes, trimmed

25 g (1 oz) butter or margarine

15 ml (1 tbsp) plain flour

300 ml ($\frac{1}{2}$ pint) vegetable or chicken stock

salt and freshly ground pepper

125 g (4 oz) French beans, topped and tailed

25 g (1 oz) wholemeal breadcrumbs

75 g (3 oz) Cheddar cheese, grated

1 Drain the soaked kidney beans and rinse well under cold running water. Put in a large saucepan, cover with plenty of fresh cold water and bring slowly to the boil.

2 Skim off any scum with a slotted spoon, then boil rapidly for 10 minutes. Half cover the pan with a lid and simmer for about 1$\frac{1}{2}$ hours, until the beans are tender.

3 Skin the onion and chop roughly. Slice the celery, carrots and courgettes.

4 Melt the butter in a large saucepan, add the onion and fry gently for about 5 minutes until softened. Add the celery and carrots. Cover and cook gently for 5 minutes.

5 Add the flour and cook gently, stirring, for 1–2 minutes. Remove from the heat and gradually blend in the stock. Bring to the boil, stirring constantly, then simmer for 5 minutes. Season with salt and pepper to taste.

6 Add the French beans and simmer for a further 5 minutes, then add the courgettes. Cook for a further 5–10 minutes, until the vegetables are tender but still with a bite to them.

7 Drain the kidney beans, add to the vegetables and heat through for about 5 minutes. Taste and adjust seasoning, then turn into a deep flameproof dish.

8 Mix the breadcrumbs and cheese together. Sprinkle on top of the bean mixture and brown under a preheated grill until crisp and crusty. Serve hot.

Menu Suggestion

Serve for a nutritious vegetarian main course, with nutty brown rice or wholemeal bread, and a crisp green salad.

THREE BEAN VEGETABLE CURRY

2.25*	£	308 cals

* plus overnight soaking

Serves 6

125 g (4 oz) dried red kidney beans, soaked in cold water overnight

125 g (4 oz) dried soya beans, soaked in cold water overnight

125 g (4 oz) dried black beans, soaked in cold water overnight

700 g (1½ lb) cauliflower

1 medium onion

½ green pepper, cored and seeded

450 g (1 lb) courgettes, trimmed

1 small piece of fresh root ginger

30 ml (2 tbsp) vegetable oil

125 g (4 oz) button mushrooms

30 ml (2 tbsp) plain flour

10 ml (2 tsp) granulated sugar

20 ml (4 tsp) ground coriander

10 ml (2 tsp) ground cumin

5 ml (1 tsp) turmeric

2.5 ml (½ tsp) chilli powder

15 ml (1 tbsp) tomato purée

900 ml (1½ pints) vegetable or chicken stock

salt and freshly ground pepper

1 Drain the soaked beans and rinse well under cold running water. Put the kidney beans in a large saucepan, cover with plenty of fresh cold water and bring slowly to the boil.

2 Skim off any scum with a slotted spoon, then boil rapidly for 10 minutes. Add the soya beans, half cover the pan with a lid and simmer for 30 minutes. Add the black beans and continue cooking for 1 hour, topping up with more boiling water as necessary, or until all the beans are tender.

3 Meanwhile, trim the cauliflower and divide into small florets. Skin the onion and slice thinly with the green pepper. Slice the courgettes thickly. Peel the root ginger and then crush or chop it finely.

4 Heat the oil in a large sauce-pan, add the onion and pepper and fry gently for 5–10 minutes until lightly browned. Stir in the whole mushrooms and the sliced courgettes and cook for a further 5 minutes.

5 Stir in the ginger, flour, sugar, coriander, cumin, turmeric, chilli powder and tomato purée. Cook gently, stirring, for 1–2 minutes, then gradually blend in the stock.

6 Drain the beans and add to the pan with the cauliflower. Bring to the boil, add salt and pepper to taste, then lower the heat, cover and simmer for about 20 minutes until the vegetables are tender. Serve hot.

Menu Suggestion

Serve for a vegetarian main course with a nutty pilaf or an Indian bread such as naan or chapati. A cool and refreshing yogurt and cucumber salad can be served afterwards, to refresh the palate.

MEXICAN RE-FRIED BEANS

| 0.15 | 173–260 cals |

Serves 4–6

30 ml (2 tbsp) vegetable oil

1 medium onion, skinned and finely chopped

1 garlic clove, skinned and crushed

1 green chilli, seeded and finely chopped

450 g (1 lb) cooked red kidney or pinto beans, (or 225 g (8 oz) uncooked beans, soaked overnight and cooked as in steps 1 and 2 of Red Kidney Bean Hot Pot on page 115), or two 425 g (15 oz) cans red kidney or pinto beans, drained

1 Heat the oil in a large frying pan, add the onion and fry gently for about 5 minutes until soft and lightly coloured. Stir in the garlic and chilli and cook for 1–2 minutes. Remove from heat.

2 Mash the beans in a bowl with a potato masher. Add to the frying pan with 150 ml ($\frac{1}{4}$ pint) water and stir well to mix.

3 Return the pan to the heat and fry for about 5 minutes, stirring until beans resemble porridge, adding water if necessary. Take care that beans do not burn. Serve hot.

Menu Suggestion
Serve as a filling for tortillas (Mexican pancakes), or as an accompaniment to any Mexican main course. For a vegetarian meal, Re-fried Beans taste particularly good topped with grated Cheddar cheese and served with boiled rice and a mixed salad.

> **MEXICAN RE-FRIED BEANS**
> Re-fried Beans, or *frijoles refritos*, are a popular vegetable accompaniment in Mexico. They can be re-fried, again and again, with the addition of a little more water each time.

*F*ALAFEL
(ISRAELI CHICK PEA PATTIES)

| **1.40*** | 📖 | 186–279 cals |

* plus overnight soaking and at least 1 hour chilling

Serves 4–6

225 g (8 oz) chick peas, soaked in cold water overnight

1 medium onion, skinned and roughly chopped

1 garlic clove, skinned and roughly chopped

10 ml (2 tsp) ground cumin

30 ml (2 tbsp) chopped fresh coriander or 5 ml (1 tsp) dried

1.25 ml ($\frac{1}{4}$ tsp) chilli powder

5 ml (1 tsp) salt

plain flour, for coating

1 egg, beaten

vegetable oil, for deep frying

1 Drain the chick peas and rinse well under cold running water. Put in a large saucepan, cover with plenty of fresh cold water and bring slowly to the boil. Skim off any scum with a slotted spoon, then half cover with a lid and simmer for 1 hour, or until the chick peas are tender.

2 Drain the chick peas thoroughly and place in a blender or food processor. Add the onion, garlic, cumin, coriander, chilli powder and salt. Work the mixture until smooth. (Alternatively, work the chick peas, onion and garlic in a mincer or vegetable mill, then mix in the other ingredients.)

3 With floured hands, shape the mixture into 16–18 small flat cakes. Dip them 1 at a time in the beaten egg, then coat them in more flour seasoned with salt and pepper. Chill in the refrigerator for at least 1 hour.

4 Pour enough oil into a deep frying pan to come about 2.5 cm (1 inch) up the sides. Heat until very hot, then fry the falafel in batches for about 3 minutes on each side until golden, turning once. Drain on absorbent kitchen paper while frying the remainder. Serve hot or cold.

Menu Suggestion
Falafel are sold as a snack in Israel, usually eaten stuffed into pockets of pitta bread, with salad. You too can serve them this way, or they can be served with a dip such as Hummus (page 19) or with natural yogurt.

LENTIL AND CELERY PEPPERS

1.05	427 cals

Serves 2

125 g (4 oz) red lentils

salt and freshly ground pepper

2 green peppers, about 175 g (6 oz) each

25 g (1 oz) butter or margarine

1 medium onion, skinned and finely chopped

75 g (3 oz) celery, trimmed and finely chopped

75 g (3 oz) low fat soft cheese

1 egg

1 Cook the lentils in boiling salted water for 12–15 minutes until just tender.

2 Meanwhile, halve the peppers and remove the cores and seeds. Place on a steamer and steam, covered, for about 15 minutes or until soft.

3 Melt the butter in a frying pan, add the onion and celery and fry gently for 2–3 minutes.

4 Drain the lentils and add to the onion and celery. Cook, stirring, for 1–2 minutes until heated through.

5 Remove the pan from the heat and beat in the cheese and egg with salt and pepper to taste.

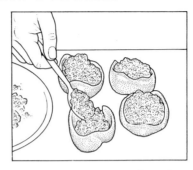

6 Remove the peppers from the steamer and fill with the mixture. Place under a hot grill for about 5 minutes or until golden brown. Serve hot.

Menu Suggestion

Serve these stuffed peppers for a tasty supper, accompanied by warm wholemeal bread and a tomato salad.

ROASTED OATMEAL VEGETABLES

1.30	260 cals

Serves 6

450 g (1 lb) medium onions

450 g (1 lb) carrots

450 g (1 lb) parsnips

120 ml (8 tbsp) vegetable oil

175 g (6 oz) coarse oatmeal

5 ml (1 tsp) paprika

salt and freshly ground pepper

1 Skin and quarter the onions, keeping the root end intact. Peel the carrots and parsnips and cut into large chunks.

2 Put the carrots and parsnips in a saucepan of water, bring to the boil and cook for 2 minutes. Drain well.

3 Heat 30 ml (2 tbsp) of the oil in the saucepan and replace the carrots and parsnips. Add the onions, oatmeal, paprika and salt and pepper to taste. Stir gently to coat the vegetables.

4 Put the remaining oil in a large roasting tin and heat in the oven at 200°C (400°F) mark 6. When very hot, add the vegetable and oatmeal mixture and baste.

5 Roast in the oven for about 1 hour, or until the vegetables are just tender and golden brown. Baste occasionally during cooking. Spoon into a warmed serving dish and sprinkle over any oatmeal 'crumbs'. Serve hot.

Menu Suggestion

These crisp, oven-fried vegetables make a welcome alternative to plainly cooked vegetables. They can be served with any traditional meat or poultry.

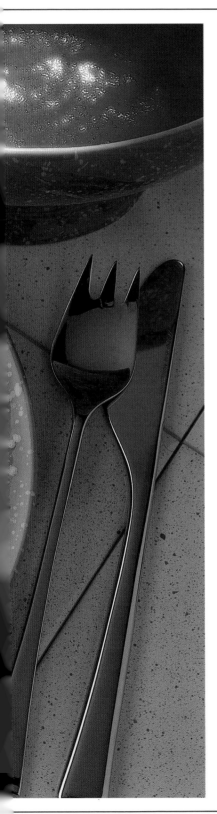

CHEESE AND NUT ROAST WITH HOT TOMATO SAUCE

| 1.10 | £ | 414–621 cals |

Serves 4–6

40 g (1½ oz) butter or margarine

1 medium onion, skinned and finely chopped

125 g (4 oz) Sage Derby cheese, or Cheddar cheese plus 5 ml (1 tsp) rubbed sage (optional)

50 g (2 oz) hazelnuts, finely chopped

50 g (2 oz) Brazil nuts, finely chopped

125 g (4 oz) unsalted peanuts, finely chopped

125 g (4 oz) fresh brown breadcrumbs

2 eggs

salt and freshly ground pepper

600 ml (1 pint) Tomato Sauce (page 149)

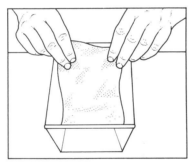

1 Using 15 g (½ oz) of the butter, grease and base-line a 900 ml (1½ pint) loaf tin.

2 Melt the remaining butter in a saucepan, add the onion and fry gently for about 5 minutes or until soft and just beginning to brown. Transfer to a bowl.

3 Grate the cheese finely into the bowl. Stir to mix with the onion, adding the sage if needed. Add the nuts, breadcrumbs and eggs and mix well again. Season to taste with salt and pepper.

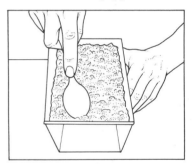

4 Press the nut mixture evenly into the prepared tin. Bake in the oven at 180°C (350°F) mark 4 for about 45 minutes, or until golden brown.

5 Leave the nut roast to cool in the tin for 2–3 minutes, then turn out on to a warmed serving dish. Cut into slices and serve hot with the tomato sauce.

Menu Suggestion

Serve this vegetarian nut roast as an alternative to roast meat or poultry. It would go well with Trio of Vegetable Purées (page 93).

BURGHUL WHEAT PILAF

| 1.00 | £ | 415 cals |

Serve 6

100–175 g (4–6 oz) butter or margarine

2 large Spanish onions, skinned and roughly chopped

2 garlic cloves, skinned and crushed

350 g (12 oz) burghul (cracked wheat)

225 g (8 oz) ripe tomatoes, skinned and finely chopped

600 ml (1 pint) vegetable stock or water

salt and freshly ground pepper

75 g (3 oz) raisins

100 g (4 oz) dried apricots, roughly chopped

50 g (2 oz) pine nuts

5 ml (1 tsp) ground cinnamon

1 Melt 100 g (4 oz) butter in a large, heavy-based saucepan or flameproof casserole. Add the onions and garlic and fry gently for about 15 minutes until softened.

2 Add the burghul and toss to mix with the onions and butter. Add the tomatoes and mix again, then pour in the stock or water and bring to the boil. Add salt and pepper to taste, then cover and cook very gently for 25 minutes.

3 Remove the pan from the heat and fold in the fruit, nuts and cinnamon, with some extra butter, if liked.

4 Cover the pan with a clean tea towel folded double, then with the lid. Leave to stand for 10 minutes.

5 To serve, taste and adjust seasoning, then spoon in a pyramid shape on a warmed serving plate or flat dish. Serve immediately.

Menu Suggestion

Cracked wheat pilaf makes the most delicious alternative to rice as a vegetable accompaniment. This version is quite rich and substantial, and would also make an unusual lunch dish served with thick and creamy Greek natural yogurt.

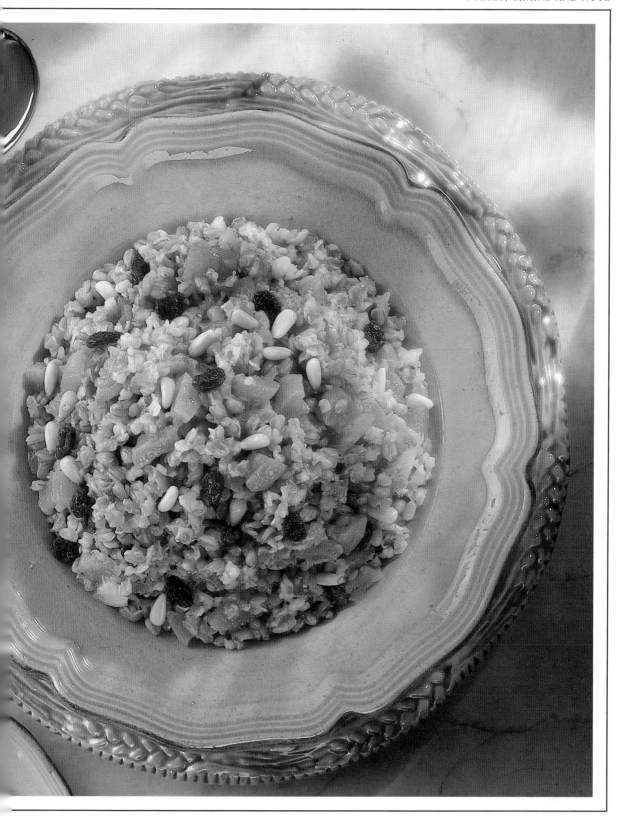

CHINESE FRIED RICE

| 0.20* | 🍴 | £ | 475 cals |

* plus 50 minutes soaking, and 2–3 hours or overnight chilling

Serves 4

350 g (12 oz) long grain rice

3 Chinese dried mushrooms, or 100 g (4 oz) button mushrooms, sliced

4 spring onions

30 ml (2 tbsp) vegetable oil

100 g (4 oz) beansprouts

100 g (4 oz) canned bamboo shoot, drained and cut into 2.5 cm (1 inch) matchsticks

100 g (4 oz) frozen peas

30 ml (2 tbsp) soy sauce

3 eggs, beaten

1 Put the rice in a sieve and wash thoroughly under cold running water until the water runs clear. Transfer the rice to a bowl, cover with cold water and leave to soak for 30 minutes.

2 Drain the rice and put in a medium saucepan. Cover with enough cold water to come 2.5 cm (1 inch) above the rice. Bring to the boil, cover tightly and simmer the rice very gently for 20 minutes. Do not stir.

3 Remove the pan from the heat, leave to cool for 20 minutes, then cover with cling film and chill in the refrigerator for 2–3 hours or overnight.

4 When ready to fry the rice, put the dried mushrooms in a bowl, cover with boiling water and leave to soak for about 20 minutes or until soft.

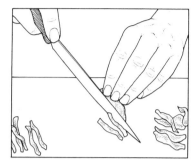

5 Squeeze out any excess moisture from the mushrooms, then cut into thin slivers. Cut the spring onions diagonally into 2.5 cm (1 inch) lengths.

6 Heat the oil in a wok or deep, heavy-based frying pan over high heat. Add all the vegetables and stir fry for 2–3 minutes. Add the soy sauce and cook, briefly, stirring.

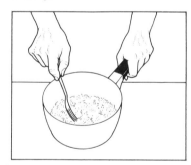

7 Fork up the rice, add to the pan and stir fry for 2 minutes. Pour in the beaten eggs and continue to stir fry for 2–3 minutes, or until the egg has scrambled and the rice is heated through. Serve immediately.

Menu Suggestion
Fried Rice can be served in individual bowls with chopsticks, as an accompaniment to any Chinese main course.

BROWN RICE RISOTTO

| 1.15 | 411 cals |

Serves 4

2 medium onions, skinned

1 medium green pepper, cored and seeded

45 ml (3 tbsp) vegetable oil

1 garlic clove, skinned and crushed

275 g (10 oz) long grain brown rice

pinch of saffron or 5 ml (1 tsp) ground turmeric

600 ml (1 pint) vegetable or chicken stock

salt and freshly ground pepper

chopped fresh parsley, to garnish

freshly grated Parmesan cheese, to serve

1 Slice the onions and green pepper finely. Heat the oil in a medium flameproof casserole, add the onions, pepper and garlic and fry gently for about 5 minutes until soft.

2 Put the rice in a sieve and wash it thoroughly under cold running water until the water runs clear. Drain well.

3 Add the rice with the saffron or turmeric to the pan. Fry gently, stirring, for 1–2 minutes until the rice is coated in oil.

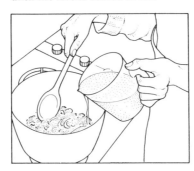

4 Stir in the stock, then add salt and pepper to taste. Bring to the boil, then cover the casserole tightly with its lid.

5 Cook in the oven at 170°C (325°F) mark 3 for about 1 hour or until the rice is tender and the stock absorbed. Taste and adjust seasoning and garnish with plenty of parsley. Serve hot, with the grated Parmesan cheese.

Menu Suggestion
Serve risotto for a first course as the Italians do, or serve for a supper dish with a colourful salad such as Crisp Endive with Orange and Croûtons (page 64).

BROWN RICE RISOTTO
Saffron threads are the dried stigmas of the saffron crocus, and saffron is said to be the most expensive spice in the world. The threads will give this dish a subtle colour and delicate flavour. Take care if substituting turmeric; it is more pungent so use it sparingly.

Useful Information
and
Basic Recipes

Know your Vegetables

From the commonplace to the exotic, vegetables need to be treated with care. Here are some hints on how to choose and store them.

BUYING AND STORING VEGETABLES

When buying vegetables always choose them carefully and make sure that they are not already old or wilted. Buy little and often to ensure freshness.

Vegetables, like fruits, can be grouped in families and each family needs to be treated in a certain way.

Brassicas and leafy vegetables, which include broccoli, sprouts, cauliflower, cabbages and spinach, don't keep well; 1–2 days in a cool, airy place, 3 days if wrapped in paper and refrigerated.

The **onion** family, which comprises leeks, garlic, shallots and spring onions, need to be chosen carefully. Make sure onions are firm, dry and not sprouting; check that the base of leeks is firm. Onions and garlic can sometimes be bought in strings. They are best stored in a cool, airy place, whereas leeks and spring onions should be wrapped in paper and refrigerated.

Pods and seeds—these are all the beans, peas, okra and sweetcorn. For the best flavour buy peas and beans as young as possible. Okra should be bought with an unmarked skin. Sweetcorn should be clean and green with silky, yellow tassels and plump, tightly packed kernels. Store peas and beans in a cool place or wrap in paper and refrigerate for 1–2 days. (If you shell peas keep them covered in the refrigerator.)

Roots and tubers, like potatoes, swedes, carrots and celeriac, should be bought firm and unwrinkled. If you buy potatoes ready washed in polythene bags it is best to transfer them to a paper bag so that they do not become soft and spongy. Store all these vegetables in a cool, airy place, such as a vegetable rack, so that air can circulate round them.

Stalks and shoots, like celery, artichokes, asparagus and fennel, should be crisp and fresh and any leaf tops should be fresh and

Celery keeps fresh if kept in water

green. Keep them wrapped in paper in the refrigerator or upright in a jug of water.

Nowadays many different types of **mushrooms** are available — button, flat cap and oyster are a few of them. Dried ones like porcini can be bought at delicatessens. Fresh ones should have unblemished skins and should be stored in paper in the refrigerator. As they deteriorate they darken in colour, so make sure they are fresh looking.

Salad leaves, like lettuce, chicory and watercress, should be bought as fresh as possible and unwrinkled. Inspect inner as well as outer leaves as the inner ones can sometimes be slimy. Apart from Iceberg lettuces, which are crisp and firm, most salad leaves do not keep well. Always refrigerate lettuce. You can wash it and dry it well and store it for 1–2 days in the refrigerator in a polythene bag.

Some vegetables are known as vegetable fruits; these include: tomatoes, courgettes, aubergines, avocados, cucumber, peppers and olives. All should be bought with unblemished skins. Tomatoes and avocados can be bought under-ripe and left to ripen.

UNUSUAL VEGETABLES

You may have come across vegetables that you would love to buy but simply don't know what to do with them. Here are some guidelines on how to treat the more unusual ones.

Artichokes, globe: to serve whole, cut off the stalk to make base level, and pull off tough, outer leaves. Tips of leaves may be

Trim the leaf tips off artichokes

trimmed off: cut off about 2.5 cm (1 inch) from the top and snip off the points of the remaining leaves round the sides. To prevent browning, cover in acidulated water. Chokes can be removed before or after cooking: spread the top leaves apart and pull out the central cone of small leaves. Scrape out the hairy choke with a teaspoon and discard, leaving the heart exposed. The heart is considered a delicacy and may be served on its own.

After preparation, globe artichokes take 20–40 minutes to cook in a large pan of boiling salted water until a leaf pulls away easily, then drain upside down. They can also be braised whole, or cut into quarters and the choke removed.

Artichokes, Jerusalem: peel the skin like potatoes, and cover immediately in acidulated water to prevent discoloration. If they are very knobbly and difficult to peel,

scrub them well in water and cook until tender. The skins should then peel away more easily.

Asparagus: wash carefully and trim off woody ends of stalks so that they are all the same length. If the stems are very woody, they can be scraped from tip to base with a sharp knife. Tie the spears in bundles with all the heads together. The bundles can be cooked upright in a special asparagus steamer or tall saucepan or, alternatively, lying down in a wide pan. Pour over boiling water and simmer for 10–15 minutes until tender.

Cardoon: similar to the globe artichoke plant, but cultivated for its leaf stalk which looks like overgrown, greyish-green celery. Trim off the fibrous skin, which is prickly at the ridges. Use raw like celery, or cook like artichokes in acidulated water.

Celeriac: peel, then cut into dice or julienne strips (see under Techniques—page 133). Immerse immediately in acidulated water to prevent browning. Large roots can be quite tough to peel, so it may be easier to cut into slices before peeling. Celeriac can also be eaten grated raw, dressed with lemon juice or vinaigrette dressing.

Fennel: trim off stalks and feathery leaves and reserve for garnish. Wash and trim away any brown bits. Cut into wedges lengthways, or slice crossways. Serve cooked or raw.

Kale: separate leaves from stems, cutting out coarse mid-ribs at base of leaves. Wash well and cut into pieces. Cook as for cabbage.

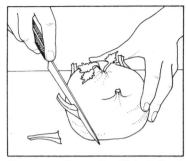

Trim sprouting stalks off the bulb

Kohlrabi/Cabbage Turnip: cut off sprouting stalks around the bulb and trim off the base. Peel, then slice or dice as required, or leave small ones whole. May also be peeled after cooking if preferred. Cook and eat as for turnips.

Okra: wash well, then trim but do not remove the stems (if the seeds inside are exposed, okra lose their shape during cooking and the sticky juices run out). Okra can be sliced into rings (seeds, too) before cooking, or for adding to stews.

Pumpkin and Squash: cut in half and then into wedges. Scoop out the seeds and cut the flesh into cubes for cooking. Small squash can be halved and baked.

Salsify/Scorzonera/Black Salsify: scrub well and trim off the root end. Peel or scrape off the skin, cut into pieces and immediately immerse in acidulated water to prevent browning. If the skin is difficult to peel, wash before cooking, then peel after cooking.

Seakale: trim the roots and wash the stalks. They can be tied in bundles and cooked like asparagus to serve hot or cold.

Seakale Beet/Swiss Chard is prepared and cooked like spinach, although the stalks can be cooked separately like asparagus.

Sweet Potatoes/Yams/Taro Cassava: peel, chop and cook like potatoes. They can also be baked in their jackets.

Preparation Techniques and Equipment

Vegetables are versatile and can be prepared in a number of different ways to add flavour, texture and colour to dishes. Here are some hints on how to prepare a range of vegetables to get the most out of them.

PREPARATION TECHNIQUES

Whether they are to be served raw or cooked, most vegetables need very simple preparation: after thorough cleaning they can be cut to the desired shape and size. However, some vegetables need special attention or a special technique for a particular effect.

CHOPPING
To chop an onion, cut in half lengthways and place on a board with the cut side down. With a very sharp, pointed knife, make horizontal cuts not quite through the length of the onion. Cut down

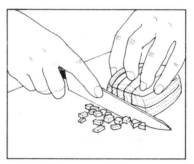

Cut across onions to make cubes

the length of the onion, then follow with downwards cuts across the onion to make cubes. The number of cuts made each way will determine how coarsely or finely chopped the onion will be.

Large, firm vegetables such as cabbages are easier to chop if they

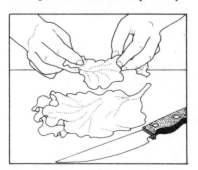

Chop leafy vegetables in layers

are first cut in halves or wedges before cutting lengthways and then across.

Large leafy vegetables can be chopped by placing several leaves on top of each other before cutting.

To chop small leafy vegetables and herbs very finely, first chop or shred the leaves on a large board. With a large, sharp knife, hold down the point with your other hand while chopping quickly with a pivotal action across the

Chopping fresh herbs finely

vegetable. Turn the board at right angles and chop in the same way, repeating until the leaves are finely chopped.

DÉGORGEING
This technique removes the juices from watery vegetables which may be bitter, e.g. aubergines and cucumbers.

1 Cut the vegetables into slices about 5 mm ($\frac{1}{4}$ inch) thick, or according to the recipe. Place in a colander, sprinkling each layer with salt.

2 Cover the slices with a plate, place heavy weights on top and leave to drain for 30 minutes, until the juices have seeped out of the vegetable. Rinse well to remove the salt and bitter juices, then dry with absorbent kitchen paper.

DICING

1 Cut slices either lengthways or across the vegetable to the same thickness as the desired cube, which may be large or small. Cut each slice into sticks.

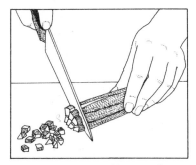

Cutting sliced vegetable into cubes

2 Cut across the sticks to make cubes (some smaller vegetables may be kept whole by careful handling until the final cuts into cubes).

GRATING

Vegetables can be grated finely or coarsely, depending on the grating blade used. Usually used for salads and in some oriental dishes.

JULIENNE

These are strips of vegetable that are matchstick shape and size. Cut the vegetable into thin slices the size of a matchstick. Cut the slices

Trim julienne strips to length

into thin sticks, then trim to the desired length.

PREVENTING DISCOLORATION

Some vegetables such as avocado pears and Jerusalem artichokes turn an unpleasant brown colour on contact with the air once they have been peeled or prepared. Acid in the form of lemon juice will prevent them from browning if sprinkled or brushed over the cut surfaces immediately after cutting.

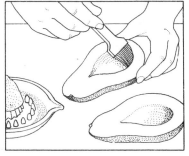

Brush lemon juice over cut avocados

Covering the cut vegetable immediately with cling film will also help prevent browning. If the vegetable is to be served in a salad it may be tossed in a dressing made with lemon juice or vinegar. Vegetables that are going to be cooked may be immersed in water that has been acidulated with a little lemon juice or vinegar.

SHREDDING

A large, firm vegetable like a cabbage should first be cut in half, quarters or wedges. Slice across or lengthways down the vegetable to shave off thin slivers.

For leafy vegetables, place several on top of each other and roll up lengthways. Hold firmly and cut across the roll into very thin slices which will unfurl into long, thin shreds.

SKINNING

Some vegetables can be very difficult to skin, but there are several 'tricks' to make it easy.

To skin tomatoes: place in a bowl or saucepan and pour over boiling water. Leave for a few seconds, then drain and plunge into cold water. The skin should peel off easily. Alternatively, pierce the tomato on a fork and hold over the gas flame until the skin is slightly charred. Leave until cool enough to handle, then peel off.

To skin peppers: place whole or half peppers (skin side up) under a hot grill until all the skin is black and charred. Rub the skins off under cold running water. The pepper underneath will have a deliciously smoky flavour.

EQUIPMENT

For preparing vegetables, the only absolute essentials are a chopping board and selection of sharp knives. However, there are several pieces of equipment and useful gadgets that will save time and energy.

Blender/Liquidiser: will purée vegetables containing liquid and some soft pâté mixtures. Also useful for making soups, drinks, sauces, mayonnaise and dips.

Electric Mixer: useful for mixing large quantities together, e.g. pâtés and stuffings, etc. May have attachments, e.g. liquidiser.

Food Processor: it will chop, shred, slice or grate, or mix different ingredients together; it will also process raw or cooked vegetables. Very useful when preparing large quantities.

Cooking Methods

Cooking vegetables in the correct way is very important to preserve the nutrients as well as the flavour, colour and texture. There are many different methods of cooking, so choose the most appropriate method for the type of vegetable and the time and facilities available. In general, vegetables should be cooked as little as possible so that they are still crisp, and never soggy, and they should be served immediately.

HOW TO COOK

BAKING

Vegetables should be baked in a moderate oven without fat or liquid until tender. They can be cooked in their skins such as jacket potatoes, or halved and stuffed (e.g. marrows and peppers), covered or uncovered.

Suitable vegetables for baking
Tubers, onions, vegetable fruits and cabbages.

BOILING

Vegetables are cooked in boiling water in a saucepan.

Suitable vegetables for boiling
Root vegetables, tubers, onions, brassicas and leaves, vegetable fruits, pods and seeds, pulses and mushrooms.

Root vegetables are prepared and placed in a saucepan and covered with cold water. Cover the pan, bring to the boil and simmer until just tender.

All other vegetables should be added to boiling water; or place the prepared vegetables in a saucepan and pour over boiling water from a kettle. Return to the boil, cover and simmer until just tender but crisp and a bright colour.

Drain off the water and use it for sauces, stocks, soups, etc; or reduce by boiling rapidly and use to glaze the vegetables.

Steam-boiling: use the minimum amount of water and a saucepan with a tight-fitting lid so that the stalks or tougher parts of the vegetable cook in the boiling water and the more delicate tops will cook more gently in the steam. This method is especially suitable for asparagus, cauliflower and broccoli, etc.

Vegetable Purées: can be made from boiled vegetables which have been cooked until tender (but not soggy) so that they are soft enough to purée. Drain off but reserve the cooking water and purée the vegetables in a mouli-légumes or food processor, or work them through a sieve.

BRAISING

Braising is a combination of frying and stewing (boiling). The prepared vegetables are fried in a little oil or fat, then liquid such as stock, water or wine is added to come about half way up the vegetables. Cover the pan and simmer until just tender and most of the liquid has evaporated. Towards the end of the cooking time it may be necessary to uncover the pan and boil the liquid to reduce it.

An alternative method of braising is to place the vegetables in a casserole after frying, add a little liquid, then cover and bake in a moderate oven until tender. This method is suitable for vegetables which are firmer and take longer to cook, and are eaten with their liquid.

Suitable vegetables for braising
Root vegetables, tubers, stalks and shoots.

FRYING

Shallow Frying: vegetables are cooked in an uncovered frying pan in a small amount of hot oil or butter (or a combination of the two). They are turned until golden brown and cooked through. If liked, they can be dusted in seasoned flour before cooking.

Sauté: firm vegetables such as potatoes are par-boiled then thoroughly drained and dried before frying to a crisp, golden brown.

Stir frying: an excellent method for cooking vegetables

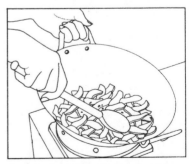

Stir-frying thinly sliced vegetables

quickly so that they retain their colour, flavour and crisp texture. The vegetables are cooked in a little oil over high heat in a wok or large heavy pan, turning all the time until just tender and crisp. Often used in oriental cooking, but preparation is time-consuming as vegetables should be thinly and evenly sliced to cook quickly.

Suitable vegetables for shallow frying

Onions, courgettes, aubergines, Chinese leaf, root vegetables and tubers, pods.

Deep Frying: vegetables are cooked in oil in a deep-fat frier or heavy saucepan. The temperature of the oil varies according to individual vegetables and recipes, but is usually 180°C (350°F) or until a cube of stale bread browns in 1 minute. Except for chips, vegetables are usually coated in flour or batter or egg and bread-crumbs. Place the vegetables in a

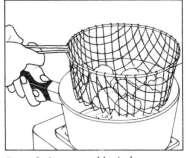

Deep frying vegetables in batter

frying basket or slotted spoon and lower into the hot oil. Cook until golden brown and crisp on the outside and just tender in the middle.

Suitable vegetables for deep frying

Onions, potatoes, aubergines, courgettes, cauliflower and mushrooms.

GRILLING

Vegetables may be cooked under a moderate grill or on a barbecue until browned and crisp on the outside, tender in the centre. They may be brushed with oil or topped with a knob of butter and

Grilling vegetables and kebabs

sprinkled with herbs, spices and seasonings first. Firmer vegetables may need to be par-boiled before grilling. Skewer on to kebab sticks to turn over easily.

Suitable vegetables for grilling

Vegetable fruits, but not avocados or small mushrooms.

PRESSURE COOKING

Very useful for reducing the cooking time and therefore more economical on fuel. With the increased pressure, the water boils at a higher temperature and there-fore cooks the food more quickly. An ideal cooking method for vegetables that normally take a long time to cook, e.g. potatoes, old root vegetables, pulses, etc. but care must be taken with other vegetables as it is very easy to overcook them. Follow manufacturer's instructions carefully for individual vegetables.

Suitable vegetables for pressure cooking

Old root vegetables, tubers, pulses.

ROASTING

Vegetables may be roasted in fat in a hot oven, or placed round a roast joint of meat until golden brown and crisp on the outside and tender inside. Firm vegetables such as potatoes may be par-boiled, then drained and dried before roasting.

Suitable vegetables for roasting

Root vegetables, tubers.

STEAMING

All vegetables which are suitable for boiling can also be cooked in steam over rapidly boiling water. This method takes a little longer than boiling, but preserves the nutrients and texture of the vegetables better. Special steamers

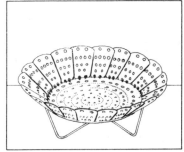

Collapsible steamers fit any pan

are available, otherwise use a saucepan with a tight-fitting lid and fit a collapsible steamer inside, or improvise with a sieve or colander to hold the vegetables. A pressure cooker without the weights is also ideal. Several vegetables may be steamed at once. Layer them up, placing the vegetables that take the longest to cook at the bottom of the steamer, or in the boiling water.

EQUIPMENT FOR COOKING VEGETABLES

Selection of saucepans and frying
 pans
Steamer
Pressure cooker
Deep-fat frier
Wok
Casseroles
Terrines and pâté dishes
Moulds for mousses
Baking dishes: pie, gratin, soufflé,
 tartlet and quiche tins
Roasting tins
Baking trays
Kebab skewers
Colander and sieves
Slices, spatulas, draining spoons
Wooden spoons

FLAVOURINGS FOR COOKING VEGETABLES

Very young, fresh vegetables, picked straight from the garden, have enough flavour of their own when served as an accompaniment to other foods. However, there are several flavourings that add variety and interest to vegetable and vegetarian dishes.

VEGETABLE FLAVOURINGS

Onions, celery, leeks, tomatoes and garlic can be added to other vegetable dishes to give flavour, colour and texture. These may be used fresh, or dried, or as a concentrated purée such as tomato or garlic.

HERBS

Herbs can be used fresh or dried to add flavour during cooking. Use half the amount of dried herbs to fresh as dried herbs are much stronger. Some herbs

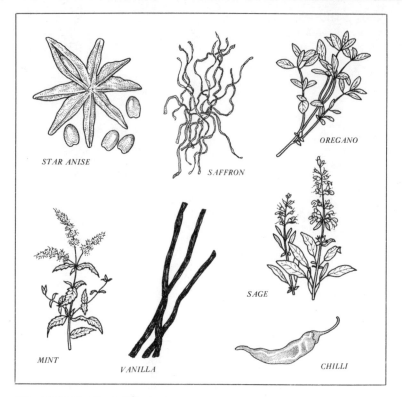

STAR ANISE
SAFFRON
OREGANO
MINT
VANILLA
SAGE
CHILLI

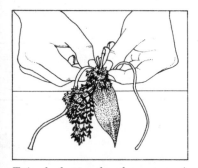

Tying herbs to make a bouquet garni

such as mint, parsley, chives and basil can be added raw to add flavour as well as garnish. A bouquet garni, which usually consists of sprigs of bayleaf, parsley and thyme tied together, can be added during cooking and removed before serving.

FLAVOURINGS FOR VEGETABLES

There are a number of flavourings that help to give variety and interest to vegetables and vegetarian dishes. For example, you can add dried vegetables, first soaked, like dried mushrooms to a dish to give it a special flavour. Flavoured oils are also useful and can turn a humdrum dish into something exotic. Try using sesame oil, this has a slightly smoky taste and is widely used in Chinese cooking. Nut oils are particularly good on salads. Flavoured vinegars used in a vinaigrette can turn an ordinary salad into something special; they are also good in marinades for vegetables. Mustard can add a spicy hotness to dishes as well as being used in vinaigrettes. Experiment with different kinds, try coarse-grained French, or the mild, sweet American kind. However, perhaps the best flavourings of all for vegetables are herbs and spices.

HERBS

These can be used fresh or dried. If you are using fresh ones, snip them into the food with scissors; if you need to chop up large quantities, as, for example, in tabbouleh, use a processor. Dried herbs are generally twice as strong as fresh so use half the quantity. Use them as a flavouring and as a garnish.

BUYING AND STORING HERBS

When buying dried herbs buy them in small quantities to ensure that they are used as fresh as possible. Store them in dark glass jars in a cool dark place to prevent them from losing their flavour.

SPICES

Spices are aromatic flavourings. They are the dried roots, barks or seeds of plants that grow mainly in hot, tropical countries.

Generally, spices are cooked with vegetables and greatly enhance their flavour. Some, like, for example, freshly ground black pepper, need not be cooked.

BUYING AND STORING SPICES

Spices are usually sold dried, either whole or ground. Although they keep for a long time, they lose their pungency of flavour quite quickly, so it is best to buy spices in small quantities.

Buy whole spices if possible and grind or crush them just before using for the best flavour. They can be bought loose, or sealed in packets or small jars.

A few spices such as root ginger can also be bought fresh from greengrocers or supermarkets, and should be stored, covered in the refrigerator.

Root ginger must be kept airtight

Dried spices should be kept airtight to seal in the flavour, and kept in a cool, dry place.

HERBS TO USE WITH VEGETABLES AND VEGETABLE DISHES

HERBS	VEGETABLES/DISHES
Basil	Tomatoes, pesto sauce
Bay	Pulses, in a bouquet garni for vegetable stocks
Bergamot	Salads
Borage	Green salads
Chervil	Vegetable soups
Chives	Potato salads, garnishes for salads
Comfrey	Salads
Coriander	Indian and Middle Eastern pulses, curried dishes and salads
Dill weed	Cucumber, salads
Fennel	Green salads
Garlic	Vegetable soups, savoury vegetable dishes
Horseradish	Dressing for potatoes and beetroot
Lemon Balm	Green salads
Lemon Grass	Salads, South Asian vegetable curries
Lemon Thyme	Herb butters, salads, marinades
Lemon Verbena	Green salads
Lovage	Vegetable soups, green salads
Marjoram	Herb butters, pulse soups, vegetable casseroles
Mint	Summer vegetable soups, new carrots, peas, potatoes, salads, as a garnish
Oregano	Tomatoes, Italian dishes
Parsley	Salads, in a bouquet garni, herb butters, as a garnish
Rosemary	Root vegetables
Sage	Salads, in a bouquet garni, herb butters, as a garnish
Savoury	Broad and French beans, salads, pulses
Sorrel	As a soup or in vegetable soups, spinach, spring greens
Sweet Cicely	Salads, dressings
Tansy	Herb butters
Tarragon	Carrots, mushrooms, salads, dressings, butters
Thyme	Tomatoes, vegetable casseroles

SPICES TO USE WITH VEGETABLES AND VEGETABLE DISHES

SPICES	VEGETABLES/DISHES
Ajowan	Curried pulses and vegetables
Allspice	Vegetable casseroles, mushroom dishes
Aniseed	Carrots, courgettes, cucumber, green salads
Asafoetida	Indian curried pulses
Caraway seeds	Cooked mushrooms, cooked cabbage, coleslaw
Cardamom pods	Curried pulses and vegetables
Cassia	Curried pulses and vegetables
Cayenne pepper	Tomato soups, curried vegetables, salad dressings
Celery seed	Coleslaw, salad dressings
Chilli powder	Pickles, vegetable curries and hot spiced vegetable dishes
Cinnamon	Indian and Middle Eastern dishes
Cloves	Stuck in onion to flavour vegetable stock
Coriander seeds	Curried vegetables, pulses, salad dressings
Cumin seeds	Indian and Middle Eastern pulse and vegetable dishes
Dill seeds	Pickling cucumber
Fennel seeds	Potatoes, salads, dressings
Fenugreek	Curried vegetables
Ginger	Chinese stir-fried dishes, Indian curries
Juniper berries	In marinades, cabbage
Laos powder	Southeast Asian vegetable dishes
Mace	Pickles
Mustard powder	Leek and celery soups, braised leeks and celery, dressings
Nutmeg	Cauliflower, spinach, white sauces
Pepper	Vegetable soups, pickles, most savoury vegetable dishes
Poppy seeds	Carrots, peas, potatoes, salads, curries
Saffron	Indian and Middle Eastern pulse and vegetable dishes
Sesame seeds	In hummus (chick-pea dip) dry-fried in salads, in salads, over vegetables au gratin
Star anise	Pickles
Turmeric	Potatoes, curried vegetables

Pulses, Grains, Nuts and Seeds

Apart from vegetables, pulses, grains, nuts and seeds form the basis of a vegetarian diet. Nowadays, they are readily available from supermarkets as well as from health shops. Here are some of the ingredients you may not as yet know but which all contribute to a nutritionally balanced diet.

PULSES

Pulse is a collective term for the dried seeds of leguminous plants (peas and beans). Pulses are extremely useful in vegetable and vegetarian cookery as they have a high nutritional content; they are especially rich in protein. Pulses are not primary proteins like meat, fish and dairy produce and do not contain all the necessary amino-acids. However, if eaten in combination with grains, a perfect protein is achieved and they make an excellent cheap and fatless substitute for meat. They are extremely versatile and can be used for making soups, salads, stews or curries.

BUYING PULSES

As they are dried, pulses make a useful store cupboard ingredient. However, although they will keep for a long time, they are best eaten within about 1 year, after which time they become tough even after lengthy cooking. It is, therefore, important to find a shop where the dried pulses are relatively fresh and stock is regularly renewed.

They are often sold loose in health-food shops and delica-tessens, and prepacked in supermarkets and grocers.

As well as in their dried form, pulses can be bought already cooked in cans, which saves considerable time in soaking and cooking, but is more expensive.

STORAGE

Pulses should be stored in a cool, dry place. They look attractive if

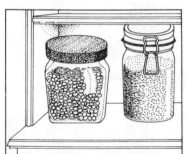

Storing pulses in dark, glass jars

stored in glass jars, but the colours tend to fade if stored in bright light. Ideally, you should store them in dark, glass jars.

Storage time depends on the quality and age of the beans, but as a general rule should not be kept more than a year for the best results.

PREPARATION

Pulses that are sold loose should be carefully picked over and any stones and grit removed; they should then be washed in several changes of cold water to remove dust. Pre-packed varieties should not need such thorough going over but should also be washed carefully.

SOAKING

Most pulses need to be soaked before cooking so that they soften and reconstitute to their original shape and size. The exceptions are split peas and lentils which can be cooked without soaking, but will cook more quickly if they have been pre-soaked.

Always soak pulses in plenty of water as they double in size and weight on soaking. Depending on the time available, they may be soaked in several ways:
Long soaking—soak in a bowl of cold water for 8–12 hours.
Short soaking—(a) place in a bowl, pour over boiling water and soak for 2 hours; (b) place in a large saucepan and pour over cold water. Bring to the boil, cook for 2 minutes, then remove from the heat, cover the pan and leave the beans to soak for 1 hour.

The soaking water should be thrown away. Place the pulses in a sieve or colander and run cold water through the pulse to wash away the impurities that can make pulses indigestible.

COOKING

Place the soaked beans in a saucepan and pour over plenty of water (add salt towards the end of cooking as this can toughen the beans). Bring to the boil and boil

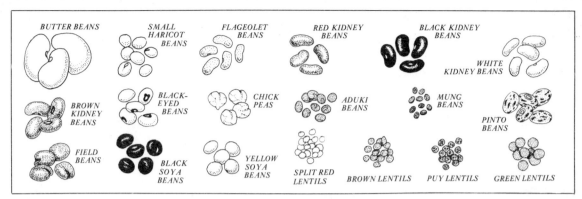

Pulses are an important source of protein in a vegetarian diet

for 10 minutes, then simmer for the required cooking time until tender. (Red kidney beans must always be boiled rapidly for 10 minutes before simmering, since they contain a toxin which can cause intestinal disturbances. This toxicity is destroyed by rapid cooking.) The cooking time will depend on the type and quality of the bean, as well as the length of soaking, and will vary from 30 minutes to 3 hours (soaked lentils will only take 10–15 minutes to cook).

Some beans will produce a scum which should be skimmed off after a few minutes boiling. Once boiled, the beans may be cooked slowly in the oven or in a slow cooker. They may also be cooked in a pressure cooker, but instructions should be followed carefully.

GRAINS

Grains are a valuable addition to vegetable dishes and a vegetarian diet in that they provide variety as well as nutritional content. Eaten in combination with pulses, grains provide the ideally balanced protein meal.

Some grains, like rice, may be familiar, but there are others, like for example, buckwheat, which are less familiar and equally delicious.

BARLEY

Barley is now more widely used for brewing than eating, but is still popular in certain parts of the world, including Scotland.

Pot barley is the whole grain with only the outer husk removed. It needs to be soaked before several hours of cooking to make it tender. It is served like rice as an accompaniment to savoury dishes or added to stews.

Pearl barley is the polished grain with the hull removed. This reduces the nutritional content but makes it easier to cook.

Barley meal/Barley flour are ground from pot and pearl barley, respectively. They contain no gluten, but can be added to wheat flour for making bread.

CORN

'Corn' is sometimes used as a generic term for all grains, but is more specifically applied to maize. There are numerous varieties of corn and it comes in various forms:

Hominy is hulled, dried corn. It can be bought dried, or ready cooked in cans, or ground into 'grits', which are served as a breakfast cereal. The whole grain can be served as an accompaniment or in savoury dishes.

Cornmeal is ground from white or yellow corn, and is available in coarse and medium grinds. There are many cornmeal dishes from the United States, and the Italian dish polenta is made from it. Finely ground white cornmeal is made into Mexican tortilla.

Cornflour/Cornstarch is the white kernel of the corn finely ground into a smooth powder. It is used for thickening, in some cakes and biscuits.

OATS

Oats are a very nutritious cereal, most popular in Scottish cookery. They are rich in fats but lacking in gluten, so they cannot be made into breads.

Oatmeal comes in 3 grades: coarse (pin-head), medium and fine. Medium oatmeal is traditionally made into porridge. Coarse oatmeal is added to soups and stews, and the fine is used for baking cakes and biscuits. The coarser the meal, the longer it will take to cook.

Rolled oats/oatflakes/porridge oats have been steamed and flattened between rollers which makes them quicker to cook than whole oats. Good for savoury crumbles or in a quiche-type pastry.

RICE

Rice is the staple diet of many countries in the world. There are thousands of varieties, but they can be divided into 3 main groups: long, medium and short grains.

Long grain rice is fluffy and separate when cooked, and is best for serving as plain boiled rice and for use in savoury rice dishes. Patna and Basmati are 2 of the best varieties to buy.

Medium and short grain rice produces a stickier, moist rice on cooking and is used for rice puddings, stuffings and risottos. Look for Carolina, Java and Italian varieties.

Brown rice is the whole grain with only the husk removed and is therefore much more nutritious than the processed white or polished rice. As a general rule, brown rice takes twice as long to cook as white rice.

Converted/Easy cook rice has been steam treated so that it cooks quickly and separates well. It is also more nutritious than white rice as the steaming is done before milling and the nutrients from the bran are included.

Ground Rice from polished rice is used for desserts and baked products.

Rice flour is finely ground to a powder, and is used for thickening as well as baking.

Wild Rice is prized for its flavour, colour and texture. Not, strictly speaking, a rice at all but a rare reed. Grown mostly in the United States, it is very expensive.

RYE

A strong-flavoured grain with a high gluten content, rye is often made into bread, particularly in Scandinavia, Germany and Russia.

Whole rye kernels need to be cracked and soaked before cooking until tender. They can be added to many savoury dishes.

Rye flour makes a heavy, brown or black loaf with a distinctive flavour. It can be mixed with wheat flour to give a lighter colour and texture. It is also used to make crispbreads.

BUCKWHEAT

Buckwheat, which is really a seed rather than a grain, has a nutty flavour and is popular in Russia and North East Europe, where it is cooked as a whole grain and also ground into flour for blinis and pancakes. In France, buckwheat is used in crêpe batter.

WHEAT

Wheat is the most common food grain to be cultivated throughout the world and is the staple food in

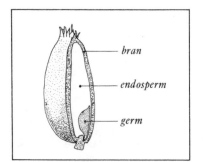

Wholewheat grain

many countries. It comes in many different forms, from the whole wheat grain to finely milled and sifted. Wholewheat flour can be made into pastry for pizzas, quiches, pies and used in bread.

Wholewheat grain must be soaked and then boiled in water for a couple of hours. It can then be eaten in the same way as rice to accompany meat, fish or vegetables, or made into a salad. It can also be boiled into a porridge like the old-fashioned 'frumenty' and served with spices and honey.

Sprinkle cracked wheat over salads

Cracked/Kibbled wheat is the whole grain cracked between rollers so that it takes less time to cook. It is eaten in the same way as wholewheat, or can be sprinkled on top of breads and salads as a crunchy topping.

Burghul/Bulgar is cracked wheat that has been hulled and par-boiled, which makes it easier to cook with a lighter texture and flavour. It can be eaten like rice or in salads. It is used in the Middle Eastern dish, tabbouleh.

Bran is the thin outer covering of the wheat grain which is removed during the refining process. It is valuable for providing extra roughage, and can be eaten raw, sprinkled on to cereals and salads or added to bread, and cake mixtures.

Wheat germ is the heart of the wheat grain and is rich in nutrients. Use like bran.

Semolina is produced during milling from the starchy part of the grain. It is often used to make milk puddings and cakes, and also for couscous and gnocchi.

Wheat flours can be divided into 2 basic types:

Hard wheat/high gluten flour grows in hot dry areas of the world and is used for making bread and pasta.

Soft wheat/low gluten flour grows in temperate climates and is used for cakes, biscuits and general use.

BUYING GRAINS

Grain products are usually bought dried and are therefore a useful store cupboard food. They do not keep indefinitely, however, and should be bought from a shop where you know there is a high turnover and the goods will be as fresh as possible and not infested by insects. They may be bought loose or prepacked.

STORAGE

Grains should be stored in a cool, dry place as they will deteriorate quickly in a warm, damp atmosphere. Prepacked grains can be stored in their packets if unopened, but once opened or if bought loose should be transferred to airtight containers such as glass or polythene.

Grains that contain fats such as oats do not keep very well as they turn rancid; they should only be kept for 1 month.

PREPARATION

Grains that are sold loose should be picked over to remove any grit, then washed. Prepacked grains should not need cleaning.

Whole grains usually need soaking in water for a few hours or overnight to soften them so that the cooking time will be reduced. Soaking varies from one type of grain to another: follow instructions on individual packets or recipes.

COOKING

The amount of cooking required depends on the type of grain and the degree of processing it has undergone, so follow individual packet or recipe instructions. The more it has been processed the less cooking it will need, and some grain products such as flakes can be eaten raw as cereals, salads or toppings.

Grains can, therefore, be served in numerous ways to provide an economical and wholesome contribution to the diet.

NUTS AND SEEDS

Nuts and seeds are a valuable food in their own right and are particularly useful in a vegetarian diet as they provide vegetable protein, fat, vitamins and minerals. They also add variety with their range of flavours and textures.

Nuts and seeds are extremely versatile and can be used raw in appetisers, snacks, salads, toppings, garnishes and cold desserts. Nuts can also be cooked into many savoury and sweet dishes such as nut pâtés and roasts for vegetarian meals, or added to vegetable, meat and fish dishes, and baked into pastries, cakes, biscuits and hot puddings. Ground nuts can also be used as a thickening agent for sauces or instead of flour in some cakes.

BUYING NUTS AND SEEDS

Fresh nuts in their shells are usually sold in greengrocers and vegetable departments of super-markets. Buy them as fresh as possible when they are new in season and still sweet and moist and heavy for their size. As they get older they will dry out and rattle in their shells.

Shelled nuts may be sold loose or already prepacked, and may be plain or roasted. They can be bought whole, halved or split, flaked, chopped or ground. Bought from grocers and super-markets they are usually blanched with the inner skins removed, but in healthfood shops they are often sold in their skins.

Some nuts such as chestnuts are preserved in cans or jars either whole or as a purée. Sesame seeds are made into a paste such as tahini, and peanut butter is made by grinding peanuts. Nuts should be bought in small quantities as their high oil content makes them deteriorate quickly.

Pumpkin, sesame and sunflower seeds are the most commonly available. They are very nutritious, being rich in minerals and vitamins. Buy in small quantities and use raw in salads or roast them.

STORAGE

Nuts and seeds should be stored in a cool, dry place to preserve the oil content as long as possible. Shelled nuts should be stored in airtight containers.

PREPARATION

Nuts in shells need to be cracked open using nut crackers, or a hammer against a hard surface.

The thin, brown, inner skin surrounding the nut kernel can be left on or removed by blanching. To blanch, pour boiling water over the nuts and leave for a few seconds or minutes (depending on the type of nut). While still warm, the skins will peel off easily, or, in

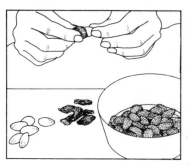

Skinning blanched almonds

the case of almonds, chestnuts and pistachios, they can be pinched between thumb and forefinger and the nuts will slip out. Hazelnuts need to be toasted until lightly browned before the skins will loosen, then they can be rubbed against each other in a bag or clean tea towel to remove the skins. Nuts such as almonds, cashews, peanuts can also be fried, toasted, roasted or grilled until golden.

Nuts can be halved, chopped or ground using a sharp knife on a chopping board. For large quantities it is quicker to use a nut mill, blender or food processor. Do not store ground nuts for they tend to go rancid quickly.

Better Health

Vegetables not only taste good but treated correctly can play an important part in keeping you healthy. Learning how to prepare and cook them is easy.

The abundance of fresh vegetables throughout the year provides an important part of our diet—not only as foods in their own right but also for adding variety, flavour and colour to meals as well as valuable nutrients.

The nutritive composition of vegetables varies considerably from one type to another, but in general vegetables are valuable for their contribution of essential minerals and vitamins, fibre, and some protein and carbohydrate.

ESSENTIAL NUTRIENTS

THE VALUE OF VEGETABLES

Food is composed of the following nutrients which the body needs to maintain health.

CARBOHYDRATE

Carbohydrate provides the body with energy, and excess carbohydrate is converted into body fat. There are 3 types of carbohydrate: sugars, starches and cellulose.

Plants form sugars in their leaves by photosynthesis (action of sunlight), then store them as starch in their stems, bulbs, roots, tubers or seeds depending on the type of plant. Therefore, carbohydrate will be found in root vegetables such as carrots, tubers (e.g. potatoes), bulbs (e.g. onions), seeds (e.g. peas, beans and pulses) and cereals.

Cellulose provides the rigid and fibrous structure of vegetables and

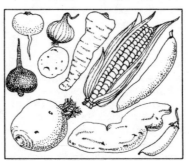

Vegetables rich in carbohydrate

cereals, but cannot be digested by man. Vegetables and cereals add valuable bulk to the diet in the form of fibre or roughage, which is essential to the digestive tract. Fibre is found in most vegetables, especially when they are eaten raw, in the husks of cereals, and in the skins, seeds and pith of fruit and vegetables.

FATS

Fats are necessary as a concentrated source of energy and form body fat for warmth and protection. They also contain the fat-soluble vitamins.

Fats contain one or more of the fatty acids: saturated, mono-unsaturated and polyunsaturated. It is the proportion of each in the fat that makes it either healthy or unhealthy.

Saturated fats are hard fats like butter, lard, processed oils and margarines, but are also present in vegetable oils like palm and coconut oil. Essentially, fats high in saturated fats are harmful. Monounsaturated fats are healthful and are found in olive oil, particularly in cold pressed virgin olive oil. Polyunsaturated fats are found in nut, seed and grain oil (like corn oil), in fish oils and some margarines high in polyunsaturated fats. Wholegrain cereals, fruits and vegetables also contain small amounts of these vital oils.

MINERALS

These are essential for the proper functioning of the body, and for growth and repair. Although there are about 15 essential minerals, only 7 elements are needed in significant amounts:

Calcium, phosphorus and magnesium are needed as constituents of bones and teeth. Green vegetables are a good source of calcium. Phosphorus and magnesium are present in most foods, and peanuts are a rich source of both these minerals. Magnesium is a constituent of chlorophyll.

Sodium, chlorine and potassium are essential for maintaining the normal balance of body fluids. Vegetables naturally contain sodium and some chlorine, and potassium is found widely in

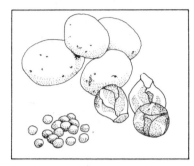

Chlorine and potassium rich foods

many vegetables such as potatoes, brassicas and peas.

Iron is present in haemoglobin in the blood, and is necessary for oxygen to be sent round the body. Iron can be stored in the body, but deficiency causes fatigue and anaemia. There is a good supply of iron in green vegetables.

PROTEIN
Protein is necessary for the growth and repair of the body, and as a secondary source of energy. Protein is made up of 22 amino-acids, and different proteins contain different numbers and combinations of these amino-acids. Proteins are divided into 2 groups:

First class/Complete proteins—contain all of the 10 essential amino-acids, and are found mainly in animal foods (meat, fish, eggs, milk and cheese).

Second class/Incomplete proteins—lack 1 or more of the essential amino-acids, and are found mainly in vegetable foods such as grains and pulses, nuts, small amounts in root vegetables and traces in green vegetables.
 If you combine one incomplete vegetable protein, such as beans, with a grain, such as wheat you would, in effect, be eating a first

class protein. This idea of combining foods to make up for each other's deficiencies is fundamental to the principles of vegetarianism.

VITAMINS
Vitamins are essential to regulate the metabolic processes and assist in utilising other nutrients. They are also important for growth, repair and protection from illness. There are two different types of vitamins: fat soluble and water soluble ones. In order for fat soluble vitamins to be absorbed by the body from foods, fats have to be eaten as well. Water soluble vitamins can only be utilised by the body in the presence of water.

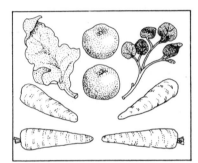

Vegetables containing carotene

Vitamin A is fat-soluble and not destroyed by normal cooking. It is necessary for growth of children, for eyesight and also protects surface tissues, e.g. hair, nails, skin and eyes etc. Vitamin A is supplied in many vegetables in the form of carotene, and is found in orange, dark green or yellow vegetables, e.g. carrots, spinach, watercress and tomatoes. The darker, outside leaves of green vegetables will contain more than the paler inside leaves.

Vitamin B is water-soluble and destroyed by prolonged cooking or drying. The B group of vitamins includes thiamine, riboflavine and nicotinic acid, and are essential links in the metabolic processes, releasing energy from other foods. Deficiency causes check in growth of children. Whole cereals and

pulses are a good source, and also potatoes and peas.

Vitamin C is water-soluble and destroyed easily by preparation, cooking and exposure to air. It is essential for growth and repair of tissues, and for resistance to infection. Extreme deficiency causes scurvy. Vegetables are a very important source of vitamin C, especially brassicas such as Brussels sprouts, cauliflower and cabbage; it is also found in parsley, watercress and tomatoes.

Vitamin D is fat-soluble and can be stored in the body. It is necessary for the absorption and laying down of calcium in bones and teeth. Vitamin D does not occur in vegetables. One of the most easily available sources of it is sunlight.

Vitamin E is fat-soluble and stored in the body. It has an effect on fertility, but is not likely to be deficient in normal diets. It is found in vegetable oils and cereal products, especially wheatgerm.

Vitamin K is fat-soluble and necessary for normal clotting of blood. It is found in vegetables such as spinach, cabbage, cauliflower and peas and also in cereals.

WATER
Although water does not provide nutrients as such, it comprises two-thirds of the body's weight and is vital to survival. Man can survive for several weeks without food, but only a few days without water.
 All vegetables have a very high water content, from about 80 to 95 per cent.

HOW TO COOK VEGETABLES FOR MAXIMUM GOODNESS

The nutritive value of vegetables is greatly reduced by storage, preservation, preparation and cooking, and therefore all vegetables should be prepared carefully to ensure that they retain as much goodness as possible.

Choose fresh vegetables which are in season and therefore at their best (and least expensive). Frozen and canned vegetables can be used, but try and avoid canned vegetables. These have often been canned and left in salty water for so long that they have lost their nutritional value.

The first essential is that vegetables should be as fresh as possible and used as soon as possible. If they must be stored for a short while, keep them correctly to prevent nutrient loss. For example, store potatoes and root vegetables in paper in a cool dark place, salad leaves in the refrigerator, and seeds and pods in the refrigerator too.

Vegetables contain more nutrients when they are raw than they do after cooking, so try to eat as many raw vegetables as possible. However, a more varied diet is possible with cooked vegetables, and some vegetables need to be cooked to make them edible and make the nutrients available, such as globe artichokes and asparagus. The main purpose of cooking vegetables is to soften the cellular tissue and to gelatinise any starch so that it can be more easily digested.

Often the tastiest and most nutritious parts of the vegetable are thrown away during preparation. The most obvious example of this wastage is the peeling of potatoes and root vegetables, as most of the nutrients are concentrated just

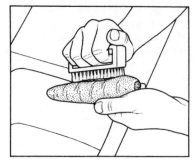

Scrub root vegetables rather than peel

below the skin and peeling removes a high proportion of the goodness. Instead of peeling, they can be well washed and scrubbed. Many other vegetables are also trimmed unnecessarily—only damaged parts, roots and tough ends need be removed. For instance, the stalks of green vegetables can be chopped and cooked with the leaves; the green tops of leeks are just as tasty as the white stems; the leaves from a cauliflower can be cooked as well as the head; and mushrooms may be wiped instead of peeled. Very young peas and broad beans can be cooked in their pods, like mangetout. Always keep the cooking liquid from vegetables, as it is the most nutritious part. A lot of the vitamins from the vegetables will have been leeched out into it. Use it for soups, stews or just drink it.

After peeling or shredding, vitamin C is rapidly destroyed by oxidation, either directly or by the action of an enzyme present in the plant tissues. This loss can be kept to a minimum by preparing vegetables immediately before use and by plunging them into boiling water at the start of the cooking process—this will destroy the enzyme. If vegetables must be prepared in advance, they should be covered immediately and kept in the refrigerator until required. Root vegetables that have been prepared can be immersed in a saucepan of cold water to prevent the air turning them brown.

During cooking, nutrients are destroyed mainly by the passage of soluble minerals and vitamins from the tissues into the cooking water, and the destruction of some vitamins by heat. Thus, some vitamin B and C are lost into the water as they are heat sensitive and water soluble. Therefore vegetables should be cooked in the

Plunge vegetables into boiling water

minimum amount of boiling water, or steamed, and the cooking water should be used, so that nutrients are not wasted. Cover the pan so that the vegetables will cook more quickly, and the ones at the top will cook in the steam. Cook vegetables for the minimum amount of time so that they are only just tender, still a bright colour and slightly crisp.

Overcooked vegetables will have less nutrients as well as being dull and soggy, and the amount of fibre will be reduced. Never add bicarbonate of soda to improve the colour as this destroys vitamin C.

Vegetables should always be served as soon as possible; keeping them warm destroys the vitamin C as well as the bright colour.

VEGETARIAN DIETS

Vegetarians are people who do not eat meat, poultry or fish. Their diet is based largely on fresh vegetables, fruit, grains, pulses, nuts and dairy produce. Some people are vegan—they eat no foods of animal origin.

Recent medical research has shown that the Western world eats too much animal fat and does not include enough fibre in the diet. A well-balanced vegetarian diet would be healthier.

However, it is very important that a vegetarian diet is well planned to ensure that the correct supply of essential nutrients is provided. Vegetarian fare may appear rather bulky and low in energy as vegetables have a high water content. The nutritional value of a vegetarian diet is very similar to that of a meat-eater, however. The main problem is to ensure that the right combinations of vegetable proteins are eaten to make up the right number of essential amino-acids. Good

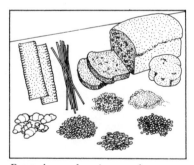

Eat pulses and grains together

combinations are cereals and pulses or cereals and nuts.

Nuts and soya beans are particularly rich in protein but for anyone to derive a primary protein from them, he/she must eat them in combination with a cereal.

Special care is needed to ensure that sufficient energy, calcium, iron and B and D vitamins are present, as these are found mainly in animal products.

Important minerals such as calcium, iron and phosphorus would have to be supplied by green vegetables and nuts.

The fat-soluble vitamins A and D are not found in vegetable fats. Vitamin A is supplied in the form of carotene from vegetables. Vitamin D could be obtained from margarine fortified with vitamin D, but since this comes from animal sources this may not be permitted. Most of the vitamin D would then have to be obtained from sunshine.

Vegetable oils, fats and margarines, and nuts provide fat in the diet, and there should be no shortage of carbohydrates or the water-soluble vitamins B and C. Vegetable extracts (e.g. Marmite) can replace meat extracts, and agar-agar seaweed can replace gelatine for setting qualities. Marmite is particularly important to the vegan since it contains vitamin B12, normally found only in meat and dairy products.

SOYA PRODUCTS

The versatile soya bean forms the base for many products which add protein to vegetarian diets.

TAMARI SAUCE

This is a natural soy sauce made only from fermented soya beans and sea salt. (The cheaper kinds of soy sauce are made from soya bean extracts and contain caramel.) Tamari sauce can be used to flavour Chinese and Japanese dishes, salad dressings, barbecue sauces and many other dishes. Buy it from health food shops and oriental grocers.

SHOYU SAUCE

This is another natural soy sauce. It is made from fermented soya beans, cracked wheat and sea salt. Available from health food shops.

MISO

This is a thick, dark brown paste, made from soya beans and grains such as whole barley or brown rice. It is high in protein and B vitamins with a flavour in many ways similar to beef extract.

Miso is used to enrich vegetable soups and stews: add only for the last few minutes of cooking.

TOFU

This is also known as soya bean curd. It is off-white in colour and available either in soft blocks or in silken form. Tofu can be bought from Chinese stores or, in its silken form, in cartons from health food shops.

Tofu provides a first class protein. It has quite low fat and carbohydrate contents and is a good source of calcium, iron and the B vitamins, thiamin and riboflavin.

SOYA MILK

Soya milk is a substitute milk made from soya beans. It is sold in cartons and cans. Soya milk can be used in the same ways as milk.

It contains protein, B vitamins, and some calcium, with no lactose or saturated fats. If possible, buy the types of soya milk that do not contain added sugar.

TEXTURED VEGETABLE PROTEIN (TVP)

This highly processed product of the soya bean is used as a meat extender or substitute.

SOYA GRITS

Also called soya splits, these are amde from cooked, cracked soya beans. In appearance, they look like small pieces of chopped soya bean. Soya grits need no soaking and will cook in 45 minutes, while providing the same nutrients as whole soya beans.

SAVA (vegan cheese)

This is an imitation hard cheese made from soya flour and a hard vegetable margarine. It is flavoured principally with yeast extract. Herb and/or garlic flavoured varieties are also available from some health food shops.

Sava is best uncooked. It can be cooked, but doesn't melt well.

Finishing Touches

All vegetable dishes must look as tempting and inviting as possible, and therefore both presentation and garnish are very important. Some vegetables, for instance, a bunch of freshly cooked asparagus, look attractive in their own right, and just need to be served 'au naturelle' to show off their beautiful shapes and colours. Other vegetables may need a little more attention to show them off to best advantage.

PRESENTATION

As vegetables are so numerous and versatile, they can be served in many different ways for a variety of occasions, including starters, main courses, vegetable accompaniments, etc. For every-day family meals, simple presentation is sufficient; for entertaining, more elaborate presentation may be necessary.

'Au naturelle' Some vegetables are attractive and colourful enough to serve as they are, completely unadorned. Other

Raw vegetables for crudités

vegetables may just need to be arranged attractively on the dish, such as a selection of raw vegetables for crudités.

Glazes A knob of butter or margarine is often placed on top of hot vegetables, which melts and forms a glaze. The butter may be flavoured with seasonings, spices, herbs or garlic, etc. Alternatively, the vegetables may be tossed in an oil such as olive oil which makes them glisten and adds flavour.

Cooking juices can also be reduced to evaporate to just a few syrupy spoonfuls, which can be spooned over the vegetables just before serving. A little alcohol, butter or other flavourings may also be added to enhance the flavour of the juices.

Aspic jelly can be used to glaze cold dishes, and is useful to prevent food from drying out.

Sauces These can be served with vegetable dishes and may be poured over just before serving or handed round separately. Hot sauces such as white, béchamel and cheese sauce go very well with vegetables, so too do mushroom, tomato and hollandaise. Salad dressings, cold sauces and mayonnaise can be served with both hot and cold vegetables.

GARNISHES

Simple garnishes give the finishing touch to many vegetable dishes. As well as being decorative, they should also be an edible accompaniment to the vegetables. The garnish can emphasise the flavour of the dish, or be a contrast in colour and texture to the vegetables.

Hot garnishes are sometimes served with hot vegetables; cold garnishes can be added to hot or cold dishes, and are quicker and easier to apply.

Selection of vegetable garnishes

HOT VEGETABLE GARNISHES

Deep-fried parsley Classic garnish which is surprisingly effective. Well-dried sprigs of parsley are deep fried until crisp.

Fried onion rings Peeled and sliced onion rings may be dusted with flour and shallow fried until golden brown. Alternatively, they can be coated in batter and deep-fried until crisp and golden.

Julienne of vegetables 'Matchsticks' of vegetables are lightly cooked and scattered over the dish. Root vegetables such as carrot, celeriac and turnip are most common (see Preparation Techniques—page 132).

Turned mushrooms Mushroom caps are carved or 'turned' into a pattern and lightly fried. Time-consuming but effective. Choose

Carving turned mushroom caps

large button mushrooms, wipe clean and trim off the stalk. On the top of the cap, make a series of curved cuts with a small sharp knife, radiating out from the centre. Take out alternate strips of mushroom to give a striped effect.

COLD VEGETABLE GARNISHES

Fresh herbs make pretty, aromatic garnishes. Use them as sprigs or whole leaves, chopped or shredded. Parsley, coriander, mint, chives and basil are some you might try.

Salad leaves Small salad leaves such as lettuce hearts, watercress, mustard and cress, chicory and endive can be used whole at the edge of a plate. Larger leaves can be made into a 'bed of lettuce' for other vegetables to be arranged on, or they can be finely shredded into strips.

Salad vegetables (vegetable fruits) Tomatoes, cucumbers and sweet peppers can be cut into various shapes and sizes to make colourful garnishes.

Tomatoes can be cut into wedges or slices for a quick and easy garnish. They can also be cut in half in water-lily shapes to garnish a large platter: cut into the centre in a zigzag pattern and then pull the 2 halves apart. A

Cutting a tomato into a water-lily

tomato rose is not as difficult as it looks: simply peel off the skin, starting at the base, in one piece round the tomato, then curl the strip of peel round and round to make a rose shape.

Cucumbers can be cut into thin slices, thicker chunks or small

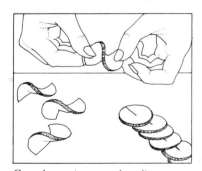

Cut, then twist cucumber slices

dice. A cucumber twist can be made by cutting into the centre of a slice and twisting the edges in opposite directions so that the slice stands up (several slices can be twisted together).

Nuts Whole or chopped nuts make a colourful and crunchy garnish for many vegetable dishes, hot and cold. Walnuts, almonds, cashews, hazelnuts, pistachios, pine nuts and peanuts can all be used.

Seeds Sprinkled over the top of vegetable dishes, sunflower and sesame seeds look very pretty and add nutritional value too. Sesame seeds are often added to Chinese stir-fried vegetables.

Red, green and yellow peppers are colourful and crunchy and can be cut into thin slices, strips or dice.

Onions Thinly sliced onions can be used for garnishing, but not for delicate vegetables as the onion flavour will penetrate. Thinly sliced leeks or spring onions can also be used for flavour as well as colour. Spring onion 'brushes' can be made by trimming off the green tops, leaving 5–7.5 cm (2–3 inches) of onion. With a sharp knife or scissors, cut lengthways down the spring onion all the way round but still attached to give a tassel shape. Leave to soak in iced water for several hours or over-night, until the cut strips curl outwards. (You can also do this with celery sticks.)

Radishes These can be cut into flowers or fans which open out in iced water like spring onions (above). Trim off the leaves, but leave any small, pretty leaves still attached. For a flower, cut down the radish almost to the stalk so that there are about 8 segments, all attached at the base. For a fan, cut thin slices all in the same direction, attached at 1 end.

147

Basic Recipes

With these basic recipes at your fingertips you can extend your repertoire of vegetable dishes. Surprise your guests with a special stuffing or start the meal with an unusual vegetable drink.

STOCK, SAUCES AND DRESSINGS

Sauces and dressings can change the whole tone of a dish.

VEGETABLE STOCK

Makes about 1.2 litres (2 pints)

30 ml (2 tbsp) vegetable oil
1 medium onion, skinned and finely chopped
1 medium carrot, washed and diced
50 g (2 oz) turnip, washed and diced
50 g (2 oz) parsnip, washed and diced
4 celery sticks, roughly chopped
vegetable trimmings such as: celery tops, cabbage leaves, Brussels sprouts leaves, mushroom peelings, tomato skins and potato peelings
onion skins (optional)
bouquet garni
6 whole black peppercorns

1 Heat the oil in a large saucepan, add the onion and fry gently for about 5 minutes until soft and lightly coloured.

2 Add the vegetables to the pan with any vegetable trimmings, outer leaves or peelings available. If a dark brown coloured stock is required, add onion skins.

3 Cover the vegetables with 1.7 litres (3 pints) cold water and add the bouquet garni and peppercorns. Bring to the boil.

4 Half cover and simmer for 1½ hours, skimming occasionally with a slotted spoon.

5 Strain the stock into a bowl and leave to cool. Cover and chill in the refrigerator. This stock will only keep for 1–2 days, after which time it will begin to go sour.

WHITE SAUCE

Makes 300 ml (½ pint) pouring sauce

15 g (½ oz) butter
15 g (½ oz) plain flour
300 ml (½ pint) milk
salt and freshly ground pepper

1 Melt the butter in a saucepan. Add the flour and cook over low heat, stirring with a wooden spoon, for 2 minutes. Do not allow the mixture to brown.

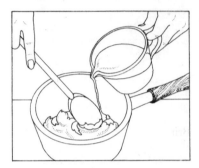

2 Remove the pan from the heat and gradually blend in the milk, stirring after each addition to prevent lumps forming.

3 Bring to the boil slowly and continue to cook, stirring all the time, until the sauce comes to the boil and thickens.

4 Simmer very gently for a further 2–3 minutes. Season the sauce with salt and freshly ground pepper.

——— VARIATIONS ———

COATING SAUCE

Follow the white sauce recipe above, but increase **butter and flour to 25 g (1 oz) each.**

CHEESE SAUCE

Follow the recipe for white sauce or coating sauce above. Before seasoning with salt and pepper, stir in **50 g (2 oz) finely grated Cheddar cheese, 2.5–5 ml (½–1 tsp) prepared mustard and a pinch of cayenne pepper.**

BÉCHAMEL SAUCE
Makes 300 ml (½ pint)

300 ml (½ pint) milk

1 slice of onion

1 bay leaf

6 black peppercorns

1 blade mace

20 g (¾ oz) butter

20 ml (4 tsp) flour

salt and freshly ground pepper

1 Put the milk into a saucepan with the onion slice, bay leaf, peppercorns and mace. Heat gently for 5 minutes, then strain.

2 Melt the butter in the rinsed-out pan. Add the flour and cook gently for 1–2 minutes, stirring. Remove pan from the heat and gradually blend in the milk. Bring to the boil, stirring and simmer for 2 minutes until thick. Season with salt and pepper.

— VARIATION —

PARSLEY SAUCE
Add **50 g (2 oz)** finely chopped **parsley** to the béchamel sauce for the 2 minutes simmering time.

HOLLANDAISE SAUCE
Makes about 150 ml (¼ pint)

60 ml (4 tbsp) white wine vinegar

6 black peppercorns

1 blade mace

1 slice onion

1 bay leaf

3 egg yolks

150 g (5 oz) unsalted butter

salt and freshly ground pepper

10 ml (2 tsp) lemon juice

30 ml (2 tbsp) single cream

1 Put the vinegar into a small saucepan with the peppercorns, mace, onion and bay leaf. Boil to reduce to 15 ml (1 tbsp). Set aside.

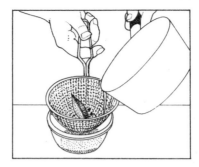

2 Beat the egg yolks in a bowl with 15 g (½ oz) butter and a pinch of salt. Strain in the vinegar.

3 Put the bowl into a saucepan of boiling water. Turn off the heat and beat in the remaining butter, in small pieces. Beat until thick.

4 Remove bowl from pan. Season to taste with salt and pepper and beat in lemon juice and cream. Serve immediately.

BASIC TOMATO SAUCE
Makes about 300 ml (½ pint)

450 g (1 lb) tomatoes, skinned and roughly chopped, or 397 g (14 oz) can tomatoes, with their juice

1 small onion, skinned and roughly chopped

1 garlic clove, skinned and chopped

1 celery stick, sliced

1 bay leaf

sprig of parsley

2.5 ml (½ tsp) granulated sugar

salt and freshly ground pepper

1 Put all the ingredients in a saucepan and bring to the boil. Simmer, uncovered, for 30 minutes until thickened. Stir occasionally to prevent sticking to the bottom of the pan.

2 Remove the bay leaf and purée the mixture in a blender or food processor until smooth, or push through a sieve using a wooden spoon. Reheat and season to taste with salt and pepper. Serve the sauce hot or cold.

QUICK TOMATO SAUCE
Makes about 450 ml (¾ pint)

397 g (14 oz) can tomatoes

5 ml (1 tsp) tomato purée

1 small onion, skinned and chopped

1 clove garlic, skinned and crushed (optional)

pinch of dried basil

pinch of sugar

freshly ground pepper

15 ml (1 tbsp) vegetable oil

1 Put all the ingredients in a blender or food processor and blend until smooth.

2 Heat in a saucepan for 10–15 minutes until slightly thickened. Serve on pasta or use in made-up dishes.

AVOCADO DRESSING
Makes about 300 ml (½ pint)

1 ripe avocado

15 ml (1 tbsp) lemon juice

30 ml (2 tbsp) mayonnaise

30 ml (2 tbsp) single cream

salt and freshly ground pepper

1 Halve, stone, peel and slice the avocado. Place in a blender or food processor with the remaining ingredients and blend at high speed until velvety smooth. Check the seasoning. Store for up to 24 hours in a screw-topped jar in the refrigerator.

GARLIC DRESSING
Makes 150 ml (¼ pint)

150 ml (¼ pint) soured cream

30 ml (2 tbsp) cider vinegar

1 large garlic clove, skinned and crushed

salt and freshly ground pepper

a pinch of sugar

1 Mix all the ingredients well together. Leave to stand for several hours before use. Store for up to 4 days in a screw-topped jar in the refrigerator.

MAYONNAISE

Makes 150 ml ($\frac{1}{4}$ pint)

1 egg yolk

5 ml (1 tsp) Dijon mustard

2.5 ml ($\frac{1}{2}$ tsp) salt

1.25 ml ($\frac{1}{4}$ tsp) freshly ground
   pepper

2.5 ml ($\frac{1}{2}$ tsp) granulated sugar

15 ml (1 tbsp) white wine or cider
   vinegar or lemon juice

about 150 ml ($\frac{1}{4}$ pint) corn or
   groundnut oil

1 Put the egg yolk into a bowl
with the mustard, seasoning,
sugar and 5 ml (1 tsp) of the
vinegar or lemon juice.

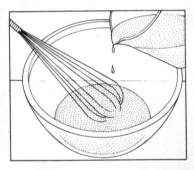

2 Mix thoroughly, then add the
oil, drop by drop, stirring
briskly with a wooden spoon the
whole time, or whisking until
sauce is thick.

3 Add a little more vinegar or
lemon juice if sauce is too
thick. When all the oil has been
added, add the remaining vinegar
or lemon juice gradually and mix
thoroughly.

4 The dressing can be stored for
2–3 weeks in a screw-topped
jar in the refrigerator.

Thinning mayonnaise
Thin mayonnaise with a little
warm water, single cream, vinegar
or lemon juice just before serving.
Add the extra liquid slowly —too
much will spoil the consistency.

AÏOLI
(GARLIC MAYONNAISE)

Makes about 300 ml ($\frac{1}{2}$ pint)

4 garlic cloves, skinned

1.25 ml ($\frac{1}{4}$ tsp) salt

2 egg yolks

300 ml ($\frac{1}{2}$ pint) olive oil

30 ml (2 tbsp) lemon juice

1 Crush the garlic cloves to a
smooth paste with a little salt.
Place in a mortar or bowl. Add the
egg yolks and remaining salt and
beat well with a pestle or spoon.
Gradually beat in the oil, a drop at
a time, until the mixture is thick
and smooth.

2 When all oil is added, add
remaining lemon juice to taste.
The dressing can be stored for up
to 4 days in a screw-topped jar in
the refrigerator.

THOUSAND ISLAND DRESSING

Makes 150 ml ($\frac{1}{4}$ pint)

150 ml ($\frac{1}{4}$ pint) mayonnaise

15 ml (1 tbsp) chopped stuffed
   olives

5 ml (1 tsp) finely chopped onion

1 egg, hard-boiled, shelled and
   chopped

15 ml (1 tbsp) finely chopped green
   pepper

5 ml (1 tsp) chopped fresh parsley

5 ml (1 tsp) tomato purée

1 Mix together the mayonnaise
with all the remaining ingredients until they are well combined.

VARIATIONS

Different types of mayonnaise can
be made by adding the following
ingredients to 150 ml ($\frac{1}{4}$ pint)
mayonnaise.

CAPER MAYONNAISE
Add **10 ml (2 tsp) chopped
capers, 5 ml (1 tsp) chopped
sweet peppers** (also known as
pimientos) and **2.5 ml ($\frac{1}{2}$ tsp)
tarragon vinegar**.

CELERY MAYONNAISE
Add **15 ml (1 tbsp) chopped
celery** and **15 ml (1 tbsp)
snipped fresh chives**.

CUCUMBER MAYONNAISE
Add **30 ml (2 tbsp) finely
chopped cucumber**.

HERB MAYONNAISE
Add **30 ml (2 tbsp) snipped
chives** and **15 ml (1 tbsp)
chopped parsley**.

PIQUANT MAYONNAISE
Add **5 ml (1 tsp) tomato
ketchup, 5 ml (1 tsp) chopped
stuffed olives** and **a pinch of
paprika**.

TOMATO MAYONNAISE
Add **half a tomato, skinned
and diced, 1 spring onion,
chopped**, and **5 ml (1 tsp) white
wine vinegar or lemon juice**.

LEMON MAYONNAISE
Add the **finely grated rind of
1 lemon** and use **lemon juice**
instead of vinegar.

CURRY MAYONNAISE
Add **5 ml (1 tsp) curry powder**
to egg yolk mixture before adding
the oil.

GREEN MAYONNAISE
Blanch **3 large spinach leaves**
quickly in boiling water, drain and
chop finely. Add to the
mayonnaise with **15 ml (1 tbsp)
chopped parsley** and **30 ml
(2 tbsp) snipped chives**.

**WATERCRESS
MAYONNAISE**
Add **one quarter of a bunch of
watercress, very finely
chopped**, to 150 ml ($\frac{1}{4}$ pint) lemon
mayonnaise.

VINAIGRETTE (FRENCH DRESSING)

Makes about 125 ml (4 fl oz)

90 ml (6 tbsp) olive or vegetable oil or see below

30 ml (2 tbsp) wine, cider or herb vinegar or see below

2.5 ml ($\frac{1}{2}$ tsp) granulated sugar

2.5 ml ($\frac{1}{2}$ tsp) mustard (e.g. wholegrain, Dijon, French or mustard powder)

salt and freshly ground pepper

1 Put the ingredients in a bowl or screw-topped jar and whisk or shake together until well blended. The oil separates out on standing, so whisk or shake again before use.

2 The dressing can be stored in a bottle or screw-topped jar for several months in the refrigerator.
Note
If a dressing calls for 150 ml ($\frac{1}{4}$ pint) dressing, add an extra 15 ml (1 tbsp) oil to the quantities given above.

VARIATIONS

FRESH HERB VINAIGRETTE

Add **15 ml (1 tbsp)** chopped fresh parsley, **15 ml (1 tbsp)** chopped fresh mint or **10 ml (2 tsp)** snipped chives, or a mixture of all three.

CURRY VINAIGRETTE

Add **5 ml (1 tsp)** curry powder to the basic vinaigrette.

MUSTARD VINAIGRETTE

Add an extra **15 ml (1 tbsp) mustard**.

GARLIC VINAIGRETTE

Add **2 garlic cloves, skinned and crushed**.

Try also **tarragon vinegar** in dressing for tomatoes or potatoes; **thyme vinegar** with eggs or mushrooms; **cider vinegar** with fruits. **Lemon juice** can be substituted for vinegar as well.
Sunflower oil alone or half and half with **olive oil** is pleasant. **Walnut oil** adds interest to strongly flavoured ingredients.

PESTO

(BASIL, GARLIC AND PINE NUT SAUCE)

Makes about 300 ml ($\frac{1}{2}$ pint)

50 g (2 oz) fresh basil leaves

2 garlic cloves, skinned

30 ml (2 tbsp) pine nuts

salt and freshly ground pepper

50 g (2 oz) freshly grated Parmesan cheese

100 ml (4 fl oz) olive oil

30 ml (2 tbsp) double cream

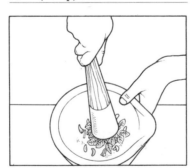

1 Grind the basil, garlic, pine nuts and salt and pepper with a pestle and mortar until a paste is formed.

2 Add the cheese and blend well. Transfer to a bowl and beat in the oil, a little at a time, stirring vigorously with a wooden spoon.

3 When all the oil has been added, fold in the cream. Serve cold, with freshly cooked pasta.

Note: The sauce can be stored for up to 2 weeks in a screw-topped jar in the refrigerator.

VARIATION

To make in a blender or food processor, put the basil, garlic, pine nuts, seasoning and olive oil in the blender or food processor and blend at high speed until very creamy. Transfer the mixture to a bowl, fold in the cheese and cream and mix thoroughly.

BLUE CHEESE DRESSING

Makes about 350 ml (12 fl oz)

150 ml (¼ pint) mayonnaise

150 ml (¼ pint) soured cream

75 g (3 oz) blue cheese, crumbled

5 ml (1 tsp) wine or cider vinegar

1 garlic clove, skinned and crushed

salt and freshly ground pepper

1 Mix all the ingredients well, with salt and pepper to taste. Allow to stand for several hours.

SOURED CREAM DRESSING

Makes 150 ml (¼ pint)

150 ml (¼ pint) soured cream

30 ml (2 tbsp) white wine vinegar

¼ small onion, skinned and finely chopped

2.5 ml (½ tsp) sugar

5 ml (1 tsp) salt

freshly ground pepper

1 Mix together the soured cream, vinegar, onion and sugar. Season and mix well.

STUFFINGS

Stuffings add interest and bulk to dishes.

CHESTNUT STUFFING

Serves 8–10

225 g (8 oz) can whole unsweetened chestnuts, drained

25 g (1 oz) butter or margarine

2 medium onions, skinned and chopped

350 g (12 oz) fresh breadcrumbs

75 g (3 oz) shredded suet

5 ml (1 tsp) lemon juice

salt and freshly ground pepper

1 Chop the chestnuts roughly. Melt the butter in a frying pan, add the onions and fry until soft but not coloured.

2 Remove from the heat and stir in the chestnuts, breadcrumbs, suet, lemon juice and salt and pepper to taste. Use as required.

CELERY AND APPLE STUFFING

Serves 6–8

50 g (2 oz) butter or margarine

100 g (4 oz) bacon, rinded and chopped

4 medium onions, skinned and chopped

4 celery sticks, trimmed and chopped

700 g (1½ lb) cooking apples, peeled, cored and sliced

175 g (6 oz) fresh breadcrumbs

60 ml (4 tbsp) chopped fresh parsley

sugar, to taste

salt and freshly ground pepper

1 Melt the butter in a frying pan, add the bacon and fry for 2–3 minutes, until golden brown. Remove from the pan with a slotted spoon and put in a bowl.

2 Fry the onions and celery for 5 minutes, then remove from the pan with the slotted spoon and add to the bacon.

3 Fry the apples for 2–3 minutes, until soft, then add to the bowl.

4 Stir in all the remaining ingredients and mix well together. Season well and use as required.

RICE STUFFING

Serves 4

50 g (2 oz) long grain rice, cooked

1 medium onion, skinned and chopped

50 g (2 oz) raisins

50 g (2 oz) almonds, blanched and chopped

30 ml (2 tbsp) chopped fresh parsley

25 g (1 oz) butter or margarine, melted

salt and freshly ground pepper

1 egg, beaten

1 Combine all the ingredients in a bowl, except the egg, then season. Add sufficient egg to bind. Use as required.

—————— VARIATIONS ——————

1 celery stick, washed and finely chopped, to replace the onion.
30 ml (2 tbsp) chopped fresh coriander, to replace the parsley.
Use brown rice instead of white.

MUSHROOM STUFFING

Serves 4

25 g (1 oz) butter or margarine

100 g (4 oz) mushrooms, wiped and chopped

1 small onion, skinned and chopped

15 ml (1 tbsp) chopped fresh parsley

salt and freshly ground pepper

100 g (4 oz) fresh breadcrumbs

1 egg, beaten

1 Melt the butter in a saucepan, add the mushrooms and onion and fry gently for 2–3 minutes, until soft but not coloured.

2 Add the parsley, seasoning and breadcrumbs and mix together well, then bind with a little beaten egg. Use as required.

SAGE AND ONION STUFFING

Serves 6–8

50 g (2 oz) butter or margarine

450 g (1 lb) onions, skinned and chopped

10 ml (2 tsp) dried sage

225 g (8 oz) fresh breadcrumbs

125 g (4 oz) medium oatmeal

salt and freshly ground pepper

1 Melt the butter in a saucepan, add the onions and sage and fry for 4–5 minutes. Stir in the breadcrumbs.

2 Toast the oatmeal under the grill for a few minutes, then stir into the breadcrumb mixture and season well. Cool before using as required.

BRAZILIAN STUFFING

Serves 4

30 ml (2 tbsp) olive oil

1 small onion, skinned and chopped

1 small garlic clove, skinned and finely chopped

$\frac{1}{2}$ a green pepper, seeded and chopped

2 tomatoes, skinned and chopped

25 g (1 oz) sultanas

4 olives, stoned and sliced

50 g (2 oz) brown rice, cooked

salt and freshly ground pepper

1 Heat the oil in a frying pan, add the onion and cook for 3–4 minutes, until soft.

2 Add the remaining ingredients and cook for about 10 minutes until they start to mash together. Use as required.

HERB STUFFING

Serves 4

50 g (2 oz) bacon, rinded and chopped

45 ml (3 tbsp) shredded suet

100 g (4 oz) fresh white breadcrumbs

15 ml (1 tbsp) chopped fresh parsley

30 ml (2 tbsp) chopped fresh mixed herbs or 10 ml (2 tsp) dried mixed herbs

grated rind of $\frac{1}{2}$ a lemon

1 egg, size 6, beaten

salt and freshly ground pepper

milk or stock, to bind

1 Fry the bacon in its own fat without browning and drain it on absorbent kitchen paper.

2 Mix it with the remaining ingredients, moistening with enough milk or stock to bind the mixture. Use as required.

POTATO DISHES

Potatoes are vesatile and can be made into dishes in their own right.

GRATIN DAUPHINOIS
(FRENCH POTATO, CREAM AND CHEESE GRATIN)

Serves 6

1.4 kg (3 lb) old floury potatoes, peeled

1 garlic clove, skinned and crushed

300 ml ($\frac{1}{2}$ pint) single cream

salt and freshly ground pepper

pinch of grated nutmeg

100 g (4 oz) Gruyère cheese, grated

1 Cut the potatoes into small pieces and parboil for 5 minutes; drain well and place in a lightly greased pie dish or shallow casserole.

2 Stir the garlic into the cream, with the nutmeg and salt and pepper to taste. Pour this seasoned cream over the potatoes and sprinkle with the cheese.

3 Cover with foil and bake in the oven at 180°C (350°F) mark 4 for about 1½ hours. Remove the foil and put the gratin under a preheated hot grill to brown the cheese.

SAUTÉ POTATOES

Serves 4

700–900 g ($1\frac{1}{2}$–2 lb) old floury potatoes, washed

salt and freshly ground pepper

50 g (2 oz) butter or 60 ml (4 tbsp) vegetable oil

1 Cook the potatoes in boiling salted water for 15 minutes or until just tender. Drain well.

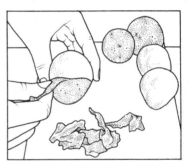

2 Remove the skin from the potatoes and cut the flesh into 0.5 cm ($\frac{1}{4}$ inch) slices with a sharp knife.

3 Heat the butter or oil in a large frying pan and add the potato slices. Cook until golden brown and crisp all over. Drain well on absorbent kitchen paper and sprinkle with salt and pepper before serving.

DUCHESSE POTATOES

Serves 6

900 g (2 lb) floury potatoes

salt and freshly ground pepper

50 g (2 oz) butter or margarine

pinch of grated nutmeg

2 eggs, beaten

1 Cook the potatoes in boiling salted water for 15 minutes or until just tender. Drain and mash. Beat in butter with nutmeg and salt and pepper. Gradually beat in eggs, reserving a little for glazing.

2 Cool the potato mixture then spoon into a piping bag fitted with a large star nozzle. Pipe the mixture in pyramids on to a greased baking sheet.

3 Brush carefully with the remaining egg to which a pinch of salt has been added. Bake in the oven at 200°C (400°F) mark 6 for about 25 minutes or until golden brown and set.

ROAST POTATOES

Serves 4

700–900 g (1½–2 lb) old floury potatoes, peeled

25 g (1 oz) lard or dripping

1 Cut the potatoes into even-sized pieces, place them in boiled salted water. Cook for 2–3 minutes and drain.

2 Heat lard in a roasting tin in the oven. Add the potatoes, baste with the fat and cook at 220°C (425°F) mark 7 for 45 minutes or until golden brown.

*S*ALADS

Whether cooked or raw, salads make a welcome contribution to any meal.

POTATO SALAD

Serves 6

900 g (2 lb) waxy potatoes

4 spring onions, trimmed and chopped

salt and freshly ground pepper

150 ml (¼ pint) Mayonnaise (page 150)

snipped fresh chives, to garnish

1 Quarter any large potatoes and put the potatoes in boiling salted water, and cook for about 15 minutes or until tender. Drain, remove the skins and leave until quite cold.

2 Cut the potatoes into small dice and place in a bowl. Add the onions to the potatoes and season with salt and pepper.

3 Stir the mayonnaise into the potatoes and toss gently. Leave the salad to stand for at least 1 hour so that the flavours can blend. To serve, sprinkle with snipped chives.

WALDORF SALAD

Serves 4

450 g (1 lb) eating apples

juice of 1 lemon

5 ml (1 tsp) sugar

150 ml (¼ pint) Mayonnaise (page 150)

½ head celery, trimmed and sliced

50 g (2 oz) walnuts, chopped

1 lettuce

few walnut halves, to garnish (optional)

1 Core the apples, slice one and dice the rest. Dip the slices in a little of the lemon juice to prevent discoloration of the fruit.

2 Toss the diced apples in the remaining lemon juice, the sugar and 15 ml (1 tbsp) mayonnaise. Leave to stand for about 30 minutes.

3 Just before serving, add the sliced celery, chopped walnuts and the remaining mayonnaise. Toss the ingredients together.

4 Serve in a bowl lined with lettuce leaves, and garnish with the apple slices and a few walnut halves, if liked.

CAESAR SALAD

Serves 4

1 large garlic clove, skinned and crushed

150 ml ($\frac{1}{4}$ pint) olive oil

75 g (3 oz) stale white bread

1 lettuce

salt and freshly ground pepper

30 ml (2 tbsp) lemon juice

25 g (1 oz) grated Parmesan cheese

8 anchovy fillets, drained and chopped

1 egg

1 Add the garlic to the oil and leave to stand for 30 minutes. Cut the stale white bread into 0.5 cm ($\frac{1}{4}$ inch) dice.

2 Heat a little of the garlic oil in a frying pan and fry the bread until golden brown on all sides. Remove with a slotted spoon and drain on absorbent kitchen paper.

3 Carefully wash the lettuce in cold running water. Drain it well and pat dry with absorbent kitchen paper.

4 Tear into bite-sized pieces and place in a salad bowl. Pour over the remaining garlic oil and toss until the leaves are completely coated. Season well with salt and pepper to taste.

5 Add the lemon juice, cheese, anchovies and croûtons and toss well to mix.

6 Boil the egg for 1 minute only, crack into the salad and give the salad a final toss. Serve immediately.

SALADE NIÇOISE
(FRENCH TUNA AND VEGETABLE SALAD)

Serves 4

198 g (7 oz) can tuna fish, drained

225 g (8 oz) tomatoes, quartered

50 g (2 oz) black olives, stoned

$\frac{1}{2}$ small cucumber, thinly sliced

225 g (8 oz) cooked French beans

2 hard-boiled eggs, shelled and quartered

15 ml (1 tbsp) chopped fresh parsley

15 ml (1 tbsp) chopped fresh basil

150 ml ($\frac{1}{4}$ pint) Garlic Vinaigrette (page 151)

8 anchovy fillets, drained and halved

French bread, to serve

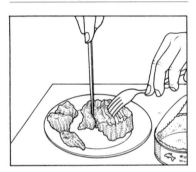

1 Flake the canned tuna into fairly large chunks. Arrange the tuna chunks in a salad bowl with the tomatoes, olives, slices of cucumber, beans and eggs.

2 Add the parsley and basil to the garlic vinaigrette, mix well and pour dressing over salad.

3 Arrange the anchovy fillets in a lattice pattern over the salad and allow to stand for 30 minutes before serving. Serve with crusty French bread.

GREEN SALAD

Use 2 or more green salad ingredients such as lettuce, mustard and cress, watercress, endive, chicory, peppers, cucumber, cabbage, etc.

1 Wash and drain the ingredients well. Just before serving, toss lightly in a bowl with French dressing (page 151), adding a little finely chopped onion if liked.

2 Sprinkle with chopped fresh parsley, chives, mint, tarragon or other herbs, as available.

TOMATO SALAD

Serves 6

700 g ($1\frac{1}{2}$ lb) ripe tomatoes, skinned

135 ml (9 tbsp) olive oil

45 ml (3 tbsp) wine vinegar

1 small garlic clove, crushed

30 ml (2 tbsp) chopped fresh parsley

salt and freshly ground pepper

1 Slice the tomatoes thinly and arrange on 6 individual serving plates. Put the oil, vinegar, garlic, parsley and salt and pepper in a bowl or screw-topped jar and whisk or shake well together. Spoon over the tomatoes.

2 Cover the plates tightly with cling film and chill in the refrigerator for about 2 hours.

COLESLAW

Serves 8

½ white cabbage, trimmed and finely shredded

1 large carrot, peeled and grated

1 large onion, skinned and finely chopped

45 ml (3 tbsp) chopped fresh parsley

4 sticks celery, trimmed and sliced

salt and freshly ground pepper

200 ml (⅓ pint) Mayonnaise (page 150) or salad cream

watercress, to garnish (optional)

1 In a large bowl, combine the first 5 ingredients, tossing well together. Season the mayonnaise or salad cream well with salt and pepper, pour over the vegetables and toss until well coated.

2 Cover the salad and chill in the refrigerator for 2–3 hours before serving, garnished with watercress, if wished.

RUSSIAN SALAD

Serves 6

1 small cauliflower, trimmed

100 g (4 oz) turnips, peeled

100 g (4 oz) carrots, peeled

225 g (8 oz) potatoes, peeled

1 small cooked beetroot, skinned

2 medium tomatoes, skinned

salt and freshly ground pepper

150 ml (¼ pint) Mayonnaise (page 150)

a little lemon juice

100 g (4 oz) peas, cooked

4 gherkins, chopped

30 ml (2 tbsp) capers

6 olives and 6 anchovies, to garnish

1 Break the cauliflower into small florets and cook in boiling salted water for about 8 minutes until tender. Drain, reserving the liquid, rinse and drain again.

2 Dice the turnips, carrots and potatoes finely and cook in the same way in the reserved cauliflower cooking liquid, rinse and drain. Dice the beetroot and tomatoes, discarding the seeds.

3 Place a layer of cauliflower in a deep salad bowl and season well with salt and pepper.

4 Thin the mayonnaise with lemon juice and spread a little over the cauliflower. Layer the other vegetables, in the same way, ending with mayonnaise.

5 To serve, sprinkle the gherkins and capers over the salad and garnish with olives and anchovies.

RICE SALAD

Serves 4

225 g (8 oz) long grain rice, cooked and drained

225 g (8 oz) tomatoes, skinned and quartered

100 g (4 oz) French beans, cooked

100 g (4 oz) frozen peas, cooked

2 celery sticks, chopped

1 small eating apple, cored and chopped

10 ml (2 tsp) chopped fresh parsley

10 ml (2 tsp) snipped fresh chives

about 90 ml (6 tbsp) Vinaigrette (page 151)

1 Put the rice (which should be quite dry) into a bowl and add the tomatoes, beans, peas, celery and apple. Stir with a fork, adding the parsley and chives.

2 Add enough vinaigrette to moisten and pile into a dish to serve.

PASTRIES

Once mastered, pastry is quick and easy to make. An excellent standby for savoury and sweet dishes.

SHORTCRUST PASTRY

When a recipe requires 225 g (8 oz) pastry, this refers to the weight of the flour. When making shortcrust pastry you should use half fat to the weight of flour.

225 g (8 oz) plain flour

pinch of salt

110 g (4 oz) butter or margarine

1 Mix the flour and salt together in a bowl. Cut the butter and lard into small pieces and add to the flour.

2 Using both hands, rub the butter into the flour between finger and thumb tips until the mixture resembles fine breadcrumbs.

3 Add 30–45 ml (2–3 tbsp) chilled water all at once, sprinkling it evenly over the surface. Stir in the water with a round-bladed knife until the mixture begins to stick together in large lumps.

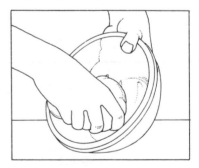

4 With 1 hand, collect the mixture together to form a ball. Knead lightly for a few seconds to give a firm, smooth dough. Do not over-handle.

5 The pastry can be used straight away, but it is better if allowed to 'rest' for about 30 minutes wrapped in foil and placed in the refrigerator.

6 When the pastry is required, sprinkle a very little flour on the work surface and on the rolling pin, not on the pastry. Roll out the pastry evenly in 1 direction only, turning occasionally. The usual thickness is about 0.3 cm ($\frac{1}{8}$ inch). Do not pull or stretch the pastry. To cook, the usual oven temperature is 200–220°C (400–425°F) mark 6–7.

WHOLEMEAL SHORTCRUST PASTRY

175 g (6 oz) plain wholemeal flour

pinch of salt

75 g (3 oz) butter or margarine

1 Mix the flour and salt together in a bowl. Cut the butter into small pieces and add to the flour.

2 Using both hands, rub the butter into the flour between finger and thumb tips until the mixture looks like fine breadcrumbs.

3 Add 30 ml (2 tbsp) chilled water all at once, sprinkling it evenly over the surface. Stir in the water with a round-bladed knife until the mixture begins to stick together in large lumps.

4 With 1 hand, collect the mixture together to form a ball. Knead lightly for a few seconds to give a firm, smooth dough. Do not over-handle.

5 The pastry can be used straight away, but it is better if allowed to 'rest' for about 30 minutes wrapped in cling film and placed in the refrigerator.

6 When the pastry is required, sprinkle a very little flour on the work surface and on the rolling pin, not on the pastry. Roll out the dough evenly in 1 direction only, turning occasionally. The usual thickness is about 0.3 cm ($\frac{1}{8}$ inch). Do not pull or stretch the pastry. To cook, the usual oven temperature is 200–220°C (400–425°F) mark 6–7.

CHOUX PASTRY

50 g (2 oz) butter or margarine

150 ml ($\frac{1}{4}$ pint) water

65 g (2$\frac{1}{2}$ oz) plain flour, sifted

2 eggs, lightly beaten

1 Put the fat and water together in a pan, heat gently until the fat has melted, then bring to the boil. Remove pan from heat.

2 Tip all the flour at once into the hot liquid. Beat thoroughly with a wooden spoon, then return the pan to the heat.

3 Continue beating the mixture until it is smooth and forms a ball in the centre of the pan. (Take care not to over-beat or the mixture will become fatty.) Remove from the heat and leave the mixture to cool for a minute or two.

4 Beat in the egg, a little at a time, adding only just enough to give a piping consistency. Beat the mixture vigorously at this stage to trap in as much air as possible. Continue beating until the mixture develops an obvious sheen, then use as required. When cooking choux pastry the usual oven temperature is 200–220°C (400–425°F) mark 6–7.

BATTER, DUMPLINGS AND TOPPINGS

FRITTER BATTER

Makes about 150 ml ($\frac{1}{4}$ pint)

75 g (3 oz) plain flour

pinch of salt

15 ml (1 tbsp) vegetable oil

1 egg white

1 Mix the flour and salt together in a bowl. Make a well in the centre and gradually mix in 90 ml (6 tbsp) water and the oil. Beat well until smooth.

2 Just before using the batter, whisk the egg white until stiff and fold into the batter.

DUMPLINGS

Makes 8

100 g (4 oz) self-raising flour

50 g (2 oz) pure vegetable fat or shredded suet

5 ml (1 tsp) chopped fresh herbs or 2.5 ml ($\frac{1}{2}$ tsp) dried (optional)

salt and freshly ground pepper

1 In a bowl, mix together the flour, suet, herbs, salt and pepper. Stir in enough cold water to give a light, elastic dough. Knead very gently until smooth.

2 Divide the pastry into 8 equal pieces and shape into balls. Add the dumplings to a casserole about 15–25 minutes before cooking is complete, then reduce the heat and cover the casserole again.

3 Simmer gently on top of the cooker or bake in the oven at 200°C (400°F) mark 6, unless otherwise stated, until the dumplings swell. Do not allow the liquid to boil or the dumplings will disintegrate.

PANCAKES

Makes 8

125 g (4 oz) plain flour

pinch of salt

1 egg

300 ml (½ pint) milk

vegetable oil

1 Mix the flour and salt together in a bowl, make a well in the centre and break in the egg. Add half the liquid. Gradually work in the flour. Beat until smooth.

2 Add the remaining liquid gradually. Beat until the ingredients are well mixed.

3 Heat a little oil in a small frying pan, running it around pan to coat sides. Raise handle side of pan slightly. Pour a little batter in from the raised side.

4 Place over moderate heat and cook until golden underneath, then turn with a palette knife and cook the other side. Slide the pancake on to a plate lined with greaseproof paper. Repeat until all the batter is used.

SAVOURY CRUMBLE

175 g (6 oz) plain flour

75 g (3 oz) butter or margarine

5 ml (1 tsp) chopped fresh herbs or 2.5 ml (½ tsp) dried mixed herbs

salt and freshly ground pepper

1 Put the flour in a bowl and rub in the butter until the mixture resembles fine crumbs. Stir in the herbs and salt and pepper to taste.

2 Sprinkle the mixture on top of a casserole and bake in the oven at 200°C (400°F) mark 6 for about 30 minutes until golden.

DRINKS

Vegetable drinks are most refreshing and nutritious.

ICED CARROT AND ORANGE JUICE

Makes 900 ml (1½ pints)

450 g (1 lb) carrots, peeled

600 ml (1 pint) fresh orange juice

soda water

1 Slice the carrots, put in a saucepan and pour in enough orange juice to cover. Cover, bring to the boil and simmer for about 20 minutes or until the carrots are tender.

2 Put the carrots and their cooking liquid in a blender or food processor and blend until smooth. Allow to cool completely, then chill in the refrigerator.

3 Add the remaining orange juice, pour into tall glasses and top up with soda water to taste.

FRESH TOMATO JUICE

Makes 450 ml (¾ pint)

900 g (2 lb) ripe tomatoes

Worcestershire sauce

lemon juice

salt and freshly ground pepper

1 Chop the tomatoes roughly, then work in a blender or food processor until puréed.

2 Press the tomato purée through a sieve into a bowl. Season to taste with Worcestershire sauce, lemon juice and salt and pepper. Pour into a jug or individual glasses.

TOMATO AND YOGURT COCKTAIL

Serves 2

4 tomatoes

150 ml (¼ pint) natural yogurt

Worcestershire sauce

lemon juice

paprika

salt

fresh mint sprigs, to garnish

1 Chop the tomatoes roughly, then purée in a blender or food processor. Press purée through a sieve into a bowl.

2 Whisk in the yogurt, then season to taste with Worcestershire sauce, lemon juice, paprika and salt.

3 Pour into tall glasses and float a sprig of mint on top of each.

VEGETABLE AND FRUIT CUP

Makes 750 ml (1¼ pints)

¼ cucumber, peeled and sliced

150 ml (¼ pint) carrot juice

300 ml (½ pint) apple juice

150 ml (¼ pint) orange juice

6 ice cubes

mint sprigs, to garnish

1 Put the cucumber, carrot and fruit juices in a blender or food processor. Add the ice cubes and blend until smooth. Pour into a jug and garnish with mint.

'OLD FASHIONED' LEMON BROSE

Makes about 300 ml (½ pint)

thinly pared rind and juice of 1 large lemon

15 ml (1 tbsp) granulated sugar

50 g (2 oz) medium oatmeal

1 Put the lemon rind and juice, sugar and oatmeal in a bowl. Pour over 300 ml (½ pint) boiling water and blend. Cover and cool.

2 When cold, strain into a jug. Refrigerate, dilute to taste.

INDEX